T0385414

# WEBER'S
# COMPLETE
# BARBECUE
# SMOKING

# WEBER'S
# COMPLETE
# BARBECUE
# SMOKING

## RECIPES AND TIPS FOR DELICIOUS
## SMOKED FOOD ON ANY BARBECUE

### JAMIE PURVIANCE

#### PHOTOGRAPHY BY TIM TURNER

# FROM THE AUTHOR

Anything smoked used to make my head swim. My confusion really started in rural Louisiana about 30 years ago, when I was a college kid on a summer road trip. One hot and humid afternoon, seductive aromas of wood-smoked pork drifted in my open car window and so, like the true carnivore I am, I followed their path to some county fairgrounds where a barbecue competition was under way. Walking among the teams of brawny cooks and their billowing barbecue rigs, including some rigs that were bigger than my car and probably twice as expensive, I wondered if I might have stumbled into a peculiar cooking cult. What exactly were these people doing with animal carcasses, foot-long meat injectors, wheelbarrows full of wood, and sauces bubbling in battered pots?

Some of the barbecue teams were selling samples, so I paid a dollar for a single sparerib. What I got was a kaleidoscope of tastes that revolved around rich, moist pork deeply nuanced with the fragrance of wood, but what in the world were all those other flavours, and how did the cooks get the succulent meat to slip so easily off the bone? There

was so much I didn't know. I just remember making involuntary sighs of appreciation and, even before I was halfway through the first rib, I asked for more.

Years went by and I continued to enjoy good barbecue and other smoked foods on occasion. I learnt a fair amount about home cooking along the way, but I assumed that the intricacies of smoked foods were still about as accessible to me as sorcery. It wasn't until I enrolled in a professional cooking school that I finally began to cut through the mystery.

It turns out that man has been smoking foods for thousands of years. It all started as a primitive way of preserving meats so they would not spoil in the hot sun, and it actually hasn't changed much since then. But our reasons for

smoking foods have changed. We do it now primarily for pleasure, not for preservation. Basically, though, smoking is still about cooking food at some distance from a smouldering fire that burns with wood.

If that sounds like barbecue to you, you are right, but smoking has always been (and still is) much bigger than barbecue's relatively narrow focus on big cuts of tough meat that require hours and hours of gentle cooking before surrendering to tenderness. I have included in this book several authentic recipes for barbecue classics, such as beef brisket, pulled pork and a version of spareribs that is reminiscent of what I ate 30 years ago in rural Louisiana. As much as I adore barbecue, I wanted to write a book about a much wider spectrum of smoked foods and I wanted to share with you many of the quickly grilled items that are improved with a little smoke. So, for example, I knew that marinated rib-eye steaks make a feast for the senses when grilled over charcoal, but why not add some wood chips to the coals and also throw in some woody sprigs of fresh thyme? Let me tell you, the results are tremendous. Unbounded by any presumptions about what can or cannot be smoked, I let my creativity run wild. I think you'll see some examples of that in recipes like Prawn and Rice Sausages with Vietnamese Dipping Sauce (see page 159) and Cedar-Planked Brie with Cherry Chutney and Toasted Almonds (see page 58). In several cases I have adapted authentic regional recipes; however, each adaptation is based on certain truths I have learnt about smoking. These truths have cleared up the mystery for me.

One of these truths is that smoke is a type of seasoning. Great cooks develop a sense about how much of any particular seasoning to use in any given dish. They learn from more experienced cooks and from cookbooks. In this book you will learn that with smoke, less is often more. In fact, the most common mistake among beginners is to use too much smoke, which turns food bitter and sooty. For each recipe in this book, I recommend a certain kind of wood and a certain length of smoking time, so please start with those recommendations. If you like a deeper smoke flavour, add a little more wood next time.

Another truth about smoking is that temperature is paramount. If you can control your fire to remain in a narrow range of heat, and if

your grill can burn wood cleanly, you are well on your way to some excellent smoked foods. But if the temperature in your grill rises and falls out of the right range, the food is bound to suffer. The fact that you can smoke food on a water smoker or a charcoal grill is so well known that I hardly need to mention it here, but I should emphasize that a gas grill is also a viable option for smoking. Why? Because nothing controls temperatures, even the very low temperatures that we often use for smoking, as easily as a gas grill. If the grill is equipped with a metal smoker box, and preferably a dedicated burner right under that smoker box, you have a reliable scenario for excellent smoking. Just set the temperature, start the wood chips burning, and position the food the right distance from the heat. For many more details on smoking on a charcoal grill, a water smoker or a gas grill, see pages 20 to 27. Everything you'll need to get started is covered there. You will see that each type of grill works differently. For instance, during long cooking sessions, a charcoal grill will require a lot more fire tending than a water smoker, but really, you can smoke food on any grill.

Many of the other truths I've learnt are included in the recipes themselves. With each one I've written special tips and instructions to help you focus on the required elements for success. In some cases, I draw your attention to a particular way of cutting meat or brining poultry prior to cooking. In other cases, the 'secret' is in how to build the fire, when to add the wood chips, or how to determine doneness. As you try more and more of the recipes, you will find

*As much as I adore barbecue, I wanted to write a book about a much wider spectrum of smoked foods and I wanted to share with you many of the quickly grilled items that are improved with a little smoke.*

that there really is no great mystery about smoking foods; there are just some simple fundamentals to follow.

I think of this book as a course that begins with the basics, helping you get past any confusion or intimidation about the topic, and then teaches you a set of skills and techniques to rely on in almost any smoked recipe. It, of course, also provides you with plenty of options for refining what you've learnt. You may start with a simple Cedar-Planked Tuna Salad (see page 170) or Oak-Roasted Leg of Lamb (see page 93), but if you are like many of us who have let a hobby turn into an obsession, it won't be long before you are tackling recipes like Brined and Maple-Smoked Bacon (see page 107), Trout and Artichoke Dip (see page 57), and Peppery Beef Jerky (see page 81). My hope is that you will emerge on the other side of this course with a thorough understanding, a fearless attitude and a greater hunger to explore the not-so-mysterious world of smoke cooking.

*Jamie Purviance*

# Table of contents

# Smoking Basics

# THE BASICS OF FIRE

At the beginning of man's history with smoking, the only real choice of fuel was wood. Today some backyard cooks still swear by this fuel, even though wood is actually pretty inefficient for cooking or smoking purposes. It often takes more than an hour for the blazing hot flames to settle down to the point where you get a good, consistent heat and, occasionally, freshly cut logs produce a dark smoke that can taint food with a sooty taste. These negatives and others have led to some excellent alternatives.

**PURE HARDWOOD CHARCOAL.**
Pure hardwood charcoal, sometimes called 'lump charcoal', is made entirely from hardwood logs that have been heated at high temperatures but with very little oxygen so they won't burn. Instead, the moisture, sap and resins in the wood are volatilized and vaporized, leaving behind only combustible carbon. The logs eventually break down into black lumps of carbonized hardwood that light faster than wood logs and maintain a relatively even range of temperatures. As hardwood charcoal burns, it releases clean wisps of aromatic smoke reflecting the type of wood used to make the charcoal. However, not all lump charcoal is the same. Look for a kind of wood you like (for example, mesquite, oak or a combination) and choose bags filled with big lumps, about the size of your fist, that clearly show real wood grain. Some brands will try to sell you 'hardwood charcoal' made from scraps of wood flooring or other building construction bits and pieces. These are not nearly as good.

**BENEFIT:** *Lights quickly and produces aromatic smoke that reflects the variety of wood used to make it.*

## HARDWOOD BRIQUETTES.

The compressed black pillows of hardwood briquettes are made from crushed pieces of hardwood charcoal. You wouldn't want to buy crushed pieces alone because they would burn out too quickly, but in hardwood briquettes those pieces are held together with a natural starch, usually cornstarch. Plus, hardwood briquettes are so densely packed that they actually burn longer and more evenly than oddly shaped lumps of hardwood charcoal that have more surface area exposed to oxygen. One reason why the briquettes are generally more popular than the lump charcoal for smoking is that they burn at predictably even temperatures. The briquettes don't create as much aromatic smoke, but it is easy enough to add wood chips or chunks to get all the smoke you want.

**BENEFIT:** *Achieves a longer, more consistent burn than pure hardwood charcoal, but with less woodsy smoke.*

## STANDARD CHARCOAL BRIQUETTES.

The most commonly available briquettes are compressed bundles of ground charcoal, coal and other materials, such as clay and limestone, along with binders like cornstarch. While they don't produce quite as much heat as pure hardwood charcoal or hardwood briquettes, smoking rarely requires high heat, and these briquettes do very well at holding steady temperatures in either a charcoal grill or a smoker. In fact, they often burn longer than hardwood briquettes. When you add wood chips or chunks to standard smouldering briquettes, you have everything you need for a first-class smoking scenario. Just one caution: briquettes that have been made with lighter fluid to help them catch fire faster can flavour your food with an oily, sooty taste. Stick with regular briquettes and light them with a chimney starter (see page 14 for more on this).

**BENEFIT:**
*Burns longer than pure hardwood briquettes and holds steady temperatures in both charcoal grills and smokers.*

## GAS.

Compared to any kind of wood or charcoal, gas has at least one advantage: it burns cleanly at the precise temperature(s) you want. As long as there's enough gas in the tank, a good gas grill will burn at almost any temperature, including the very low temperatures preferred for most smoking recipes. The smoky flavour achieved with a gas grill alone is not at all the same as what you get with wood smoke. It is the result of fats and juices dripping on to the angled metal bars that protect the burners. They vaporize and turn into their own appealing smoke. Nevertheless, a gas grill equipped with a smoker box that is filled with wood chips can easily pump out glorious clouds of wood smoke (see page 26 for more on this).

**BENEFIT:** *Provides the most precise temperatures and the cleanest burn.*

# LIGHTING CHARCOAL

First and foremost, please light your charcoal in a completely safe and reliable way. The best method is to use a chimney starter, which is a metal cylinder with a handle on the outside and a wire rack on the inside.

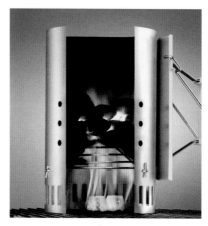

1 Begin soaking wood chips in water (it's not necessary to soak wood chunks). A disposable foil tray works well for this. Make sure the chips are almost entirely submerged in the water for at least 30 minutes.

2 Remove the cooking grate from your grill and place the chimney starter on the charcoal grate below. Place a couple of firelighters under the wire rack and fill the space above the rack with charcoal. Because most smoked recipes call for low to medium heat, you won't always need to fill the chimney completely with charcoal. Sometimes it's best to start smoking recipes with just enough charcoal to fill one-third to one-half of the chimney. Avoid using lighter fluid – you don't need it.

3 Light the firelighters. Place the filled chimney starter on top. The beauty of this method is that the chimney pushes air up through the coals, lighting them much faster and more evenly than if the coals are spread out.

If you don't have a chimney starter, you can also build a pyramid of charcoal briquettes over a few paraffin cubes, and light the cubes.

Now wait (but never leave a grill unattended). With adequate ventilation, lump charcoal will be fully lit in 15–20 minutes, briquettes in 25–35 minutes. Briquettes will develop a light coating of white ash when fully lit; lump charcoal will show white ash just around the edges. If you wait too long, either type of charcoal will disintegrate into powder.

# DIRECT (GRILLING) VERSUS INDIRECT (ROASTING) HEAT

Having enough heat is one thing, but what really matters is what you do with it. Your first decision is direct heat (grilling) or indirect heat (roasting).

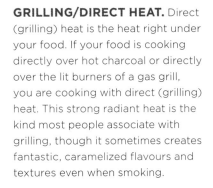

**GRILLING/DIRECT HEAT.** Direct (grilling) heat is the heat right under your food. If your food is cooking directly over hot charcoal or directly over the lit burners of a gas grill, you are cooking with direct (grilling) heat. This strong radiant heat is the kind most people associate with grilling, though it sometimes creates fantastic, caramelized flavours and textures even when smoking.

Direct (grilling) heat works well for small, tender pieces of food that cook quickly, such as hamburgers, steaks, chops, boneless chicken pieces, fish fillets, shellfish and sliced vegetables. It sears the surface of these foods, developing flavours, textures and caramelization while it cooks the food all the way to the centre.

**ROASTING/INDIRECT HEAT.** When you're not cooking food directly over the heat, or if the food is somehow shielded from direct heat, you are using indirect (roasting) heat. For example, if the coals are burning on one side of the grill and your food is smoking on the opposite side, you are using indirect (roasting) heat. If the burners on the left and right sides of your gas grill are lit, but the burners in the middle are unlit and the food is smoking in the middle, you are cooking with indirect (roasting) heat.

Indirect heat works better for larger, tougher foods that require longer cooking times, such as roasts, whole chickens and ribs. It is also the proper way to finish cooking thicker foods or bone-in cuts that have been seared or browned first over direct (grilling) heat.

**SOME OF EACH HEAT.** There are times when it's wise to cook with both direct (grilling) and indirect (roasting) heat – even when smoking. For example, you may want to start cooking bone-in chicken thighs over direct heat to sear and brown the outsides, and then move them over indirect heat/ roasting to finish. If you try to cook the thighs over direct heat only, you will probably burn the outsides before the meat in the centre is fully cooked.

The combination of two heats allows for both beautifully browned outsides and thoroughly cooked interiors. If you want to smoke those thighs, simply add wood chips to the charcoal or to the gas grill's smoker box after you move the thighs over indirect heat/roasting.

# THE BASIC EQUIPMENT

According to most food historians, the first 'smokers' were nothing more than racks of tree branches suspended high over smouldering embers to smoke and preserve whole fish and slabs of meat. Eventually cooks realized that covering the food and the fire gave them a lot more control over the temperatures and the smoke. Now backyard cooks have several good options for covered smokers. Let's open the lid on some of the most popular.

**CHARCOAL GRILL.** This one is most often associated with grilling (direct heat), but grilling and smoking are in fact very close cousins in the family of outdoor cooking. Since so many people already have a charcoal grill, they usually start their smoking adventures here. The typical approach is to create a small charcoal fire on one side of the charcoal grate, and then position the food on the opposite side of the grill (on the cooking grate). When you add wood to the charcoal and close the lid, you are smoking in every sense of the word. But that's just the beginning. Then you need to control the heat by minding the coals and adjusting the vents for the right amount of airflow. It's a live fire, and you are actively participating in how it burns.

**WATER SMOKER.** Many outdoor cooks take great pleasure in minding the coals of a charcoal grill, but smoking often requires very low temperatures, and tending a small bed of coals in a charcoal grill can be quite challenging. A water smoker eliminates the need to be as actively involved in the fire. This smoker can hold temperatures of 95–130°C/200–250°F for at least four hours, often longer, depending on the type of fuel. The Weber version is an upright, bullet-shaped unit with three sections. The charcoal and wood burn in the bottom section, which is designed with vents for controlling airflow. The water pan in the middle section acts as a shield between the charcoal and the food, which means the heat is indirect (roasting). The food sits on one or two racks above the water pan, and the top section is a domed lid, which has a thermometer and an adjustable vent.

**GAS GRILL.** You may be a bit surprised to learn that gas grills can do an excellent job of smoking foods. Actually most large-scale, commercial smoking done around the world today for favourites like smoked fish and sausages is achieved with gas smokers, because it's much easier to maintain ideal smoking temperatures. What's true for commercial smokers is also true for backyard gas grills: if you set the gas grill for the ideal temperature and burn wood chips in the grill's metal smoker box, you can smoke almost any food with top-quality results. In most cases, you will light some but not all of the burners, and then smoke the food on an area of the cooking grate not directly over a lit burner. By adjusting the temperature of the burner under the smoker box, you can control how quickly or slowly the chips release their fragrant smoke.

**OFFSET SMOKER.** This type of smoker is called 'offset' because the charcoal and wood burn inside a box (the 'firebox') that is off to the side of the main cooking chamber. This particular design prevents the cooking chamber from getting too hot. There is a baffle (or vent) on the outside of the firebox to help you control how much air is getting to the charcoal, and a baffle on top of the chimney extending above the cooking chamber so you can accelerate or decelerate how quickly air and smoke pass through the smoker. This design has evolved from basic barrel smokers of yesteryear: empty oil barrels cut in half, fitted with a cooking grate, and laid on their sides so embers and wood could burn at one end of the barrel and food could smoke at the other.

**REFRIGERATOR-STYLE SMOKER.** This smoker is for those who want to smoke more than 10 kg/22 lb of food at once. The design is similar in some respects to that of an offset smoker; that is, the firebox is situated to the side of the cooking chamber. Originally these smokers were made from old refrigerators, because they were cheap and the walls were well insulated. But the concept worked so well that some manufacturers have adapted the design to include digital technology that allows you to program the temperature, the smoking time and even the amount of smoke, often generated by little wood pellets that are slowly fed into an electric firebox for a hands-off smoking experience.

# MUST-HAVE TOOLS

### TONGS

Without a doubt, the most useful tool of all. Have at least three pairs: one for raw food, one for cooked food, and one for handling charcoal and wood. Look for heavy-duty tongs that are about 40 cm/16 inches long, feel comfortable in your hand, have sturdy metal pincers and are dishwasher safe. A locking mechanism is nice for keeping them closed when not in use.

### CHIMNEY STARTER

The simple design lets you start charcoal quickly and evenly without using lighter fluid. Look for one with two handles – one side handle for lifting and a hinged top handle for support – and a capacity to hold at least 3 kg/6½ lb of briquettes (80 to 100 pieces).

### GRILL BRUSH

Go for a sturdy, long-handled brush with stiff stainless steel bristles.

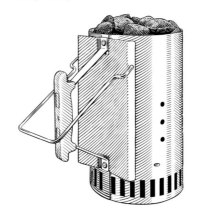

### INSTANT-READ MEAT THERMOMETER

If you want to smoke meat like a pro, this is the surest way to check for doneness. You can buy an inexpensive thermometer with a dial face or a more expensive one with a digital face. Ideally the sensor will be very close to the tip so you can easily pinpoint the area of the food you want to measure.

### INSULATED BARBECUE GLOVES

Invest in a pair with good-quality materials and workmanship that will hold up well over time.

### DISPOSABLE FOIL TRAYS

Have these to hand for soaking wood chips, creating a water pan or just moving food to and from your grill. You can cook with them, too, capturing precious juices.

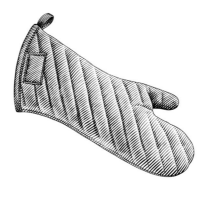

## RIB RACK

This clever item saves space on your grill by standing racks of ribs upright rather than laying them flat. Now you can smoke four racks of ribs where previously you could only smoke two.

## INJECTOR

One of the trade secrets of many barbecue champions is enhancing the meat prior to smoking with a savoury brine or marinade. This is the tool for distributing that liquid evenly inside the meat.

## SPICE SHAKER

Keep a batch of your magic seasonings in one of these shakers so that you can quickly and evenly distribute the spices with a few flicks of the wrist.

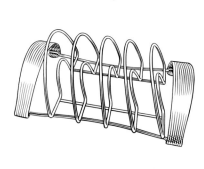

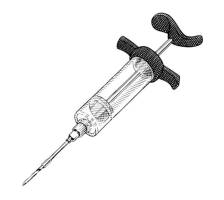

## SPRAY BOTTLE

Fill one with apple juice and vinegar for keeping smoked meats moist.

## STEEL BUCKET

Smart outdoor cooks pour their hot charcoal ashes into one of these before throwing them away. A steel bucket is also a safe place for a chimney starter filled with lit charcoal. Place only on a non-combustible surface.

## TIMER

If timing is everything, then having a good timer makes all the difference. The best ones have extra large digits for easy reading, loud alarms and the flexibility to count up from zero as well as down from whatever time you pick.

# THE SMOKE

You could power a hot air balloon around the world with all the opinions about which types of wood smoke go best with certain kinds of food.

The truth is, there is no absolute right answer. We're talking about a matter of personal taste. So if you prefer a particular type of wood with a particular kind of food, well then, that's your right answer. If you aren't sure about your favorite wood-and-food combinations, start with the suggestions on the next page and feel free to agree or disagree however you like. That's part of the sport we call barbecue.

At most stores you will find smoking wood sold either in chips or chunks. Each calls for a slightly different way of handling.

**CHIPS.** Little slivers of wood, roughly "chipped" for maximum surface area. They should almost always be soaked in water for at least 30 minutes, or they may catch fire and raise the temperature of the grill. Add to a bed of burning charcoal or to a gas grill's smoker box. A couple handfuls provide 10 to 20 minutes of smoke. Add unsoaked chips to charcoal for a short burst of flames and heat.

**CHUNKS.** These vary widely in their shape and size, some will be too big for a gas grill's smoker box, the usual size is about as big as a fist and will smoulder for a couple of hours on a bed of charcoal. Water doesn't seep into chunks any deeper than about ¼ inch. To prevent them catching fire, arrange along the outer edge of the bed of charcoal.

**PLANKS.** Flat and skinny, these boards come in several sizes, from squares barely as big as a pork chop to rectangles long enough to hold an entire side of salmon. All planks should be submerged in water for at least an hour before being charred on a grill. Place your plank onto the cooking grate (in the roasting area), close the lid for 2 minutes or until the plank begins to smoke. Place your seasoned food onto the plank, close the lid and cook until done

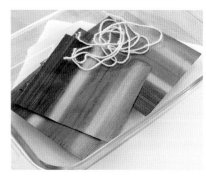

**PAPERS.** A relatively new entry onto the smoking stage, these thin pieces of wood should be submerged in water for 1-2 hours before being wrapped around whatever you want to smoke. Tie the bundles with butcher's twine, and then roast them on all sides to produce light amounts of sweet smoke.

# WOOD PLANK COOKED BURGERS

**PREP TIME:** 30 minutes
**COOKING TIME:** 10–15 minutes
Makes 4 burgers

150 g/5 oz beef mince
150 g/5 oz pork mince
¼ onion, finely chopped
1 teaspoon thyme, finely chopped
1 teaspoon parsley, finely chopped
50 g/2 oz breadcrumbs
½ egg, beaten
½ tsp salt
black pepper, to taste
oak or beech wood plank

1 Place the wood planks into water to soak, and leave for 1–2 hours.
2 Combine all of the ingredients into a mixing bowl, and mix thoroughly. Shape into 4 burgers.
3 Place into the refrigerator to chill. This will allow the burgers to hold their shape well.
4 Preheat the barbecue for a medium-high direct (grilling) heat. Add the soaked planks, and leave for 5 minutes. They should start to crackle. Brush with a little olive oil.
5 Add two of the burgers to each of the oak or beech planks. Close the lid and allow to cook for 10-15 minutes. Turn half way through.
6 Serve in a bun, with salad and Weber relish.

# WOOD PAPER BAKED PEAR & BLUEBERRIES

**SERVES 4**
**PREP TIME:** 10 minutes
**COOKING TIME:** 10 minutes

4 medium pears, cored and
    cut into 1-cm/ ½-inch chunks
150 g/5 oz blueberries
1 tablespoon honey
Weber smoking papers

1 Soak the wood papers for 1–2 hours.
2 Place the pear and blueberries into the centre of the paper. Drizzle with honey. Secure with string or a wooden skewer.
3 Place over medium, indirect (roasting) heat for 10 minutes.
4 Serve in the wood paper.

# WHAT GOES WITH WHAT?

Most cooks agree that wood smoke comes in varying strengths or intensities, from mild to moderate to strong. It's a good idea to match the intensity of the smoke to the intensity of your food. The chart on the right provides some suggestions.

Also know that you don't have to confine yourself to just one type of wood. Sometimes you can achieve the most wonderful results by mixing two or three kinds of wood together. For example, a 50/50 mix of hickory and apple produces a sweet-smelling smoke that is also hearty enough for barbecued ribs or brisket. If you want to get even more creative, consider adding one of these other options to your grill:

**Grapevines**
**Herb stems**
**Lavender branches**
**Rosemary branches**
**Soaked black peppercorns**
**Soaked cardamom pods**
**Soaked cinnamon sticks**
**Tea leaves**

**CAUTION.** It may be tempting to throw any kind of wood on to the fire, including the wood from a fallen tree in your garden, but be warned. Some wood, particularly softwoods like pine and aspen, can create bitter smoke that may in fact be toxic. And make sure any wood, herbs or vines you use have not been treated with harmful chemicals or 'finished' in some way. If it's in the smoke, it's on your food.

## WOOD TYPE

| |
|---|
| ALDER |
| APPLE |
| CHERRY |
| PEACH OR PEAR |
| BEECH |
| HICKORY |
| MAPLE |
| OAK |
| PECAN |
| MESQUITE |

| CHARACTERISTICS | PAIR WITH |
|---|---|
| **MILD:** Delicate flavour that is particularly nice with fish | Salmon, swordfish, other fish, poultry, pork |
| **MILD:** Slightly sweet but also dense, fruity smoke flavour | Beef, poultry, game birds, pork (particularly ham) |
| **MILD:** Slightly sweet, fruity smoke flavour | Poultry, game birds, pork |
| **MILD:** Slightly sweet, woodsy flavour | Poultry, game birds, pork |
| **MILD:** Sweet, delicate and arguably the most versatile of wood flavours | Fish, poultry, pork (including sausages), lamb, vegetables, cheese |
| **MODERATE:** Pungent, smoky, bacon-like flavour | Pork, poultry, beef, wild game, cheeses |
| **MODERATE:** Mildly smoky, somewhat sweet flavour | Poultry, vegetables, ham |
| **MODERATE:** An assertive but pleasing flavour; sometimes a little acidic; blends well with sweeter woods | Beef (particularly brisket), poultry, pork |
| **MODERATE:** Rich and more subtle than hickory, but similar in taste; burns cool, so ideal for very low heat smoking | Pork, poultry, lamb, fish, cheeses |
| **STRONG:** In a class by itself – a big, bold smoke bordering on bitter | Beef and lamb |

# HOW TO SMOKE ON A CHARCOAL GRILL

The most useful way to set up your charcoal grill for smoking is to create a two-zone fire. That simply means you arrange the coals on one side of the charcoal grate and leave the other side empty, giving yourself two heat zones. One will have grilling/direct heat and the other will have indirect heat/ roasting.

## TO PREPARE THE GRILL, FOLLOW THESE STEPS:

1 Before you light the charcoal, find out how much wood the recipe suggests and soak wood chips in water for at least 30 minutes so that they will smoulder and smoke rather than flame up (no need to soak wood chunks). Light the charcoal as shown on page 12. More often than not, you will need only a small bed of charcoal for smoking, so start with the chimney filled about halfway. The swinging handle above the chimney starter is there to help you lift and aim the chimney where you want it. Be sure to wear insulated barbecue gloves when handling the chimney starter.

2 Pour the lit charcoal on one side of the charcoal grate, either right on to the grate or into a charcoal basket. Put the empty chimney starter on a heatproof surface away from children and pets. If the coals are not in a charcoal basket, use long-handled tongs to arrange them so that they cover one-third to one-half of the charcoal grate. It's ok if the coals are piled one or two coals deep, but no more than that. Remember, you will probably need medium or low indirect heat/roasting, so start with a small amount of charcoal and add more later as needed.

3 For recipes that involve more than 30 minutes of cooking time, place a water pan on the empty side of the charcoal grate. Fill the pan about three-quarters full with water. The pan will catch any juices and fat from the food. Plus, the water will absorb and release heat slowly, evening out the temperatures and adding a bit of moisture to the smoking process.

Make sure to sweep away any ashes that have accumulated on the bottom of the bowl, and leave the bottom vents open all the way. Now preheat the grill.

4 Put the cooking grate in place (if the grate has hinged sides, arrange one of the hinged sides over the charcoal so that it will be easy to add more charcoal later without taking the grate off the grill). Then put the lid on the grill and open the top vent completely. Now wait until the temperature reaches the right range for the recipe you are making (see 'How Hot Should the Fire Be' on page 24). Keep in mind that as the charcoal burns, the temperature will drop. When the temperature reaches the upper end of your desired temperature range, remove the lid and use a long-handled grill brush to scrape off any bits and pieces of food that may be sticking to the cooking grate.

5 Drain and add the required amount of wood chips evenly over the charcoal. The chips should be damp but not so wet that they could put out the fire. The damp chips will initially drop the temperature of the fire, but the heat will recover once the chips begin to smoulder. Put the lid on the grill and wait for smoke to start pouring out of the grill. Open the lid and arrange the food on the cooking grate as the recipe suggests. Close the lid and position it so that the vent is on the side of the grill opposite the charcoal; this will draw the heat and smoke over the food and out of the vent.

**6** If you will be cooking for more than 30 minutes, you will probably need to add more charcoal over time. If you are using standard charcoal briquettes, add them when they are fully lit, because the taste of food sometimes suffers when it absorbs the aromas of partially lit briquettes. Fortunately, Weber briquettes and pure hardwood charcoal and hardwood briquettes don't produce any unwanted aromas in the early stages of their burning, so you can add those to the fire when they are unlit or lit.

The grill vents control the airflow. The more air flowing into the grill, the hotter the fire will grow and the more frequently you will have to replenish it. To minimize that, keep the lid closed as much as possible, but the vents on the bottom of the grill should (almost always) be left

open whenever you are cooking. To slow the rate of your fire's burn, close the top vent as much as three-quarters of the way.

All kinds of charcoal, especially briquettes made with fillers, will leave some ash after all the combustible carbon has burned. If you allow the ashes to accumulate

on the bottom of the grill, they will eventually cover the vents and starve the coals of air, eventually putting them out. So, every hour or so, give the vents a gentle sweep to clear them of ashes.

## HOW HOT SHOULD THE FIRE BE?

You will be working with five temperature ranges:

1] **High: 230–290°C/450–550°F**
2] **Medium: 180–230°C/350–450°F**
3] **Low: 130–180°C/250–350°F**
4] **Very low: 95–110°C/200–225°F**
5] **Extremely low: about 80°C/175°F**

A thermometer on the lid of the grill is the most reliable way to check the temperature. If your grill doesn't have one, you can try the 'feel the heat' method. Spread out your hand, palm down, 10 cm/ 5 inches above the charcoal grate. If you have to move your hand in 2–4 seconds, you have high heat; in 5–7 seconds, medium heat; 8–10 seconds, low heat; 11–12 seconds, very low heat; and 13–15 seconds, extremely low heat.

# HOW TO SMOKE ON A WATER SMOKER

A water smoker allows you to smoke foods at consistent temperatures below 130°C/250°F for several hours – something that is quite challenging to do with a charcoal grill. The design is basically an upright bullet made of three sections. The charcoal burns in the bottom section. The water sits in a pan in the middle section, preventing any fat from dripping on to the coals and, more importantly, keeping the temperature nice and low. Your food sits on one or two racks in the middle section. The top section is the lid, which includes a vent and a thermometer.

TO PREPARE THE SMOKER, FOLLOW THESE STEPS:

1 First of all, remove the top and middle sections from the bottom section. Lay the charcoal grate in the bottom section and set the charcoal ring on top of the grate. Fill a chimney starter to the top with charcoal and pour the charcoal into the ring, spreading it out evenly. Now, if you are using a 57-cm/22½-inch-diameter smoker, fill the chimney starter with charcoal again and light the charcoal in a completely safe and reliable way, as shown on page 12. If you are using a 47-cm/18-inch-diameter smoker, fill the chimney starter only halfway with charcoal and light it safely.

2 As soon as the briquettes are lightly covered with grey ash (or once the lump charcoal is lit round all the edges), carefully pour the lit charcoal over the unlit charcoal, spreading it out evenly. Over time the unlit charcoal will burn and extend the life of the fire.

3 Make sure the water pan is empty and suspended inside the middle section and the charcoal access door is closed. Set the middle section over the bottom section.

4 Immediately, before the water pan gets too hot, fill it about three-quarters full with water. Next, set the two cooking grates in place inside the middle section. Now place the lid on top. A water smoker has vents on the bottom section and one on the lid.

At this point open the top vent completely and close the bottom vents halfway. Wait until the smoker reaches its ideal temperature range of 110–130°C/225–250°F.

5 Open the charcoal access door and, using long-handled tongs, add as many dry wood chunks as the recipe suggests. Close the charcoal

access door and wait a few minutes for the smoke to stream out of the vent on the lid.

6 Remove the lid and arrange the food on the cooking grates, starting with the bottom grate. When you're using both grates, remember this: whatever you have on the top grate will drip on to whatever you have on the bottom grate. It might be delicious if a pork shoulder drips on to a spare rib, but not so delicious if a spare rib drips on to a whole salmon fillet.

Put the lid on the smoker. Wait for 10–15 minutes to see if the temperature returns to the ideal range (110–130°C/225–250°F). Often the food will bring down the temperature inside the smoker. If the temperature is too low, open the bottom vents a bit more. If the temperature is too high, close the top vent as much as halfway, but never close the top vent all the way.

# TENDING THE FIRE

A water smoker can maintain temperatures in the range of 110–130°C/225–250°F for several hours with no added fuel.

One of the reasons for this is the water pan. Positioned between the fire and the food, the water regulates the smoker's temperature to a certain extent by absorbing or releasing heat. The less air you allow into the smoker, the lower the temperature will go. To raise the temperature, open the bottom vents. You can also add more charcoal through the access door in the middle section, though this is rarely necessary for recipes that cook in less than four hours. The charcoal can be unlit or lit, though standard briquettes are prone to emit an acrid aroma at first, producing a taste that can spoil the fruits of your labour, so either light those briquettes first in a chimney starter, or use lump charcoal or hardwood briquettes to refuel the smoker. Open the top lid as little as possible while smoking. When no smoke is streaming out of the top vent,

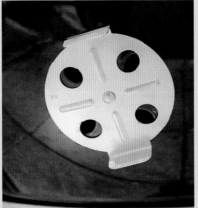

you may want to add more wood chunks to the coals below – although not too many or too often. It's easy (and awful) to overdo it. The smoke should flow like a gentle stream, not as if it is billowing out of a steam engine.

Every couple of hours, refill the water pan to maintain the proper temperature range.

# HOW TO SMOKE ON A GAS GRILL

Setting up a gas grill for smoking can be very easy, especially if the grill is equipped with a built-in smoker box; however, there is a way to create smoke even without a built-in smoker box.

First, start soaking wood chips in water (check the recipe for the amount you'll need). They should soak in water for at least 30 minutes or else they are likely to catch fire and give you more flame than smoke.

## TO PREPARE THE GRILL, FOLLOW THESE STEPS:

1 Follow all safety and lighting instructions when lighting a gas grill.

To light a gas grill, first open the lid so unlit gas fumes don't collect in the cooking box.

2 Now move the regulator level to the on/up position and wait a minute for the gas to travel through the gas line.

3 Turn on the burners, including the dedicated burner under the smoker box, setting them all to high. Close the lid and preheat the grill for 10–15 minutes.

When the temperature reaches 260°C/500°F, use a long-handled grill brush to clean the cooking grates. In most cases, you will be smoking with indirect/roasting (and usually low) heat. Turn off the burner(s) in the middle and turn down the outside burners to the suggested temperature in the recipe. For now, keep the dedicated burner under the smoker box turned to high.

5 Arrange the food in the middle of the cooking grate, over the unlit burner(s). Close the lid as soon as possible and let the food cook.

Controlling the temperature of a gas grill is not a matter of opening and closing vents, it's simply a matter of turning knobs. In most cases you will adjust one or two of the main burners during cooking, though if you want to smoke at very low temperatures (below 130°C/250°F), turn off all of the main burners and use just the dedicated burner under the smoker box for the heat. Keep in mind that most of the smoke will accumulate around the smoker box. The closer your food is to the smoker box, the more smoke flavour it will absorb. Do not place food directly over the smoker box.

Using long-handled tongs, open the lid of the smoker box. Grab some of the soaked wood chips with the tongs, let the excess water drain off, and drop the wood chips into the smoker box. Spread out the wood chips so they cover the bottom of the box, directly exposing as many chips as possible to the burner below. Continue to add as many wood chips as the recipe suggests. Close the lid of the smoker box.

4 Close the lid of the grill and wait a few minutes for smoke to pour out of the grill. Now it's time to lower the heat of the dedicated burner under the smoker box to medium or low so that the wood will smoulder slowly.

# IF YOUR GRILL DOESN'T HAVE A BUILT-IN SMOKER BOX

## MAKE YOUR OWN
Place drained wood chips in a foil tray, cover with aluminium foil, and poke holes in the foil to allow the smoke to escape. Place the tray directly on the bars over an unlit burner or two, preferably in a back corner. Put the cooking grates in place. Turn on the grill, with all the burners on high, and close the lid. When smoke appears, begin cooking your food, adjusting the temperature of the grill as needed. You can't add more chips to the tray, but at least it's a start.

## BUY ONE
Nowadays you can purchase a heavy-gauge stainless steel smoker box to sit right on top of your cooking grate. The metal will conduct the heat of your grill to the soaked wood chips you pile

inside the box. The holes in the lid will direct the fragrant smoke over your food. When the wood chips have burnt out, you can simply open the lid and add more, if you like.

# BRINGING ON EVEN MORE FLAVOUR

Whenever you smoke foods, remember that your main ingredient is like the lead singer in a rock-and-roll band. Every other ingredient, including the smoke, should make the main ingredient better.

It would be a shame to smother something inherently wonderful like a well-marbled slab of pork ribs under a blanket of spices and sauce, but even the most fabulous main ingredients can often be improved with a few judicious layers of flavour. By adding one or more of the options outlined below, you have a chance to distinguish your food with an ethnic authenticity or a creative spin that reflects your personal style. This act of layering flavours – and balancing them with the smoke for a harmonic effect – is what separates the masters from the masses.

**RUBS.** A rub is a mixture of ground spices, herbs and other seasonings, sometimes including sugar. The term comes from massaging the meat with the seasonings, but you will actually do better to sprinkle the rub over the main ingredient from a distance of 15 cm/6 inches or more so that you distribute it evenly without roughing up the surface of the main ingredient. Rubs work best when there's a little salt in the mix, because salt has a way of creating openings in the surface of the food – allowing flavours, including smoke flavours, to penetrate deeper.

**MARINADES.** Wet marinades tend to work more slowly than rubs, but over time they can seep in even further, and often their acidic elements like vinegar or citrus juices help to tenderize meats. Marinades typically include a fair amount of oil, too, which can help a lot when a particular meat, fish or vegetable lacks enough richness on its own to be smoked for a long time. Smoke compounds are fat and water soluble, so the added moisture can also help marinated foods absorb smoke a bit better.

**BRINES.** These salty solutions are really just intense versions of marinades, but their high concentration of salt means that they work on the main ingredients a little differently. The salt is able to open up pathways in the meat and carry moisture and flavours deep inside. Long periods of smoking tend to dry out meats, so brines are often effective antidotes to this concern.

**SAUCES.** Barbecue sauces, sticky glazes, savoury relishes, slow-cooked chutneys, flavoured butters, thin dipping sauces, luscious vinaigrettes … the possibilities go on and on. The world of sauces is so vast that it is hard to know which ones are best for smoked foods and how to make them. The next few pages address those important questions.

# A SMOKER'S STORE CUPBOARD

The basis of great cooking begins with ingredients. What you do with those ingredients may prove to be even more important. Hopefully you will bring time-tested techniques, your own intuition and a spark of imagination to your cooking, but first let's spell out the critical ingredients that you will use again and again when layering the flavours of smoked food. These are the most useful for making rubs, marinades, brines and sauces.

## OILS
Vegetable oil
Extra-virgin olive oil
Rapeseed oil
Toasted sesame oil

## SWEETENERS
Apple juice
Black treacle
Brown sugar
Granulated sugar
Honey
Maple syrup
Soft drinks

## TOMATO PRODUCTS
Ketchup
Tomato purée
Tomato sauce

## SAUCES AND MUSTARDS
Dijon mustard
Hoisin sauce
Soy sauce
Worcestershire sauce
Yellow mustard

## VINEGARS
Balsamic vinegar
Cider vinegar
Red wine vinegar
Rice vinegar
White wine vinegar

## OTHER
Beer
Chicken and beef stock
Cocoa powder
Horseradish
Hot pepper sauce
Liquid smoke

## DRIED HERBS
Basil
Bay leaves
Dill
Marjoram
Oregano
Parsley
Rosemary
Sage
Tarragon
Thyme

## SPICES
Allspice
Black pepper
Cayenne pepper
Celery seeds
Chinese five spice
Cinnamon
Cloves
Coriander
Crushed red chilli flakes
Cumin
Curry powder
Fennel seeds
Garlic granules
Ginger
Mustard powder
Mustard seed
Nutmeg
Onion granules
Paprika
Prepared chilli seasoning
Pure chilli powder
Sea salt
Sesame seeds
Turmeric
White pepper

# MAKING RUBS

## HOT
black pepper
cayenne pepper
crushed red chilli flakes
prepared chilli seasoning
pure chilli powder

## SWEET
allspice              cloves
brown sugar           granulated sugar
Chinese five spice    nutmeg
cinnamon

## EARTHY
caraway seeds
celery seeds
coriander
cumin
paprika

## HERBACEOUS (dried herbs)
basil         oregano
bay leaves    parsley
dill          rosemary
fennel        sage
marjoram      thyme

## SHARP
garlic granules
mustard powder
mustard seeds
onion granules
turmeric

## SALTY
fleur de sel
sea salt
smoked sea salt

# RUBS

The most interesting spice rubs have a well-orchestrated complexity. There may be several ingredients involved but no single flavour dominates the rest. With that goal in mind, when you make spice rubs for yourself, begin by choosing spices from more than a couple of the six categories pictured here, and keep in mind that each category balances with the one beside it. So, for example, hot spices such as chilli powder and cayenne pepper have an affinity for sweet elements like brown sugar and cinnamon. Similarly, earthy spices and dried herbs complement each other. The herbs tend to brighten and lighten the deep flavours of spices like cumin and paprika. And if you are using sharp spices like garlic and onion granules, try adding a bit more salt to mellow out their bite.

## HOW LONG?

If you leave a rub on for a long time, the seasonings intermix with the juices in the meat and produce more pronounced flavours as well as a crust. This is good to a point, but a rub with a lot of salt or sugar will draw moisture out of the meat over time, making the meat tastier, yes, but also drier. So how long should you use a rub? Here are some guidelines.

| TIME | TYPES OF FOOD |
| --- | --- |
| Up to 15 minutes | Small foods, such as shellfish, cubed meat for kebabs, and vegetables |
| 15–30 minutes | Thin cuts of boneless meat, such as chicken breasts, fish fillets, pork fillet, chops and steaks |
| 30 minutes–1½ hours | Thicker cuts of boneless or bone-in meat, such as leg of lamb, whole chickens and beef roasts |
| 2–8 hours | Big or tough cuts of meat, such as racks of ribs, whole hams, pork shoulders and turkeys |

# MOLE RUB

MAKES: about 4 tablespoons

2 tablespoons chilli powder
2 teaspoons cocoa powder
2 teaspoons soft dark brown sugar
1 teaspoon sea salt
1 teaspoon ground black pepper

**1** Mix the ingredients in a small bowl.

# FRENCH ROAST SPICE RUB

MAKES: about 3½ tablespoons

2 tablespoons coarsely ground French roast coffee beans
2 teaspoons sea salt
1 teaspoon soft light brown sugar
¾ teaspoon ground black pepper
½ teaspoon garlic granules

**1** Mix the ingredients in a small bowl.

# LEMON PEPPER SALT

MAKES: about 2 tablespoons
SPECIAL EQUIPMENT: spice mill

2 lemons
4 teaspoons sea salt
2 teaspoons ground black pepper

**1** Preheat the oven to 110°C/200°F/Gas Mark ¼.

**2** Using a vegetable peeler, cut strips of zest from the lemons, avoiding the white, bitter pith. Place the lemon zest on a baking sheet and bake for 30–45 minutes until dry and golden. Leave to cool.

**3** Pulverize the lemon zest in a spice mill. Transfer to a small bowl and mix with the salt and pepper. Use immediately or store in a tightly covered jar for up to 4 weeks.

# ANCHO CHILLI RUB

MAKES: about 10 tablespoons/¼ pint

3 tablespoons sea salt
2 tablespoons chilli powder
2 tablespoons soft light brown sugar
2 tablespoons garlic granules
1 tablespoon ground cumin
2 teaspoons ground black pepper

**1** Mix the ingredients in a small bowl.

# STEAK HOUSE RUB

MAKES: about 3 tablespoons
SPECIAL EQUIPMENT: spice mill

2 teaspoons black peppercorns
2 teaspoons mustard seeds
2 teaspoons paprika
1 teaspoon garlic granules
1 teaspoon sea salt
1 teaspoon soft light brown sugar
¼ teaspoon chilli powder

**1** Crush the peppercorns and mustard seed in a spice mill. Pour into a small bowl and add the remaining ingredients.

## SWEET HEAT RUB

MAKES: 5 tablespoons

2 tablespoons soft dark brown sugar
2 teaspoons ground cinnamon
2 teaspoons dried thyme
2 teaspoons sea salt
2 teaspoons ground black pepper
1 teaspoon grated nutmeg
½ teaspoon ground allspice
½ teaspoon ground mace

**1** Mix the ingredients in a small bowl.

## CHINESE FIVE SPICE RUB

MAKES: 2 tablespoons

2 teaspoons garlic granules
1 teaspoon Chinese five spice
1 teaspoon ground black pepper
1 teaspoon ground coriander
1 teaspoon sea salt

**1** Mix the ingredients in a small bowl.

## PROVENCE RUB

MAKES: 4 teaspoons

2 teaspoons herbes de Provence
1 teaspoon celery seeds
½ teaspoon sea salt
¼ teaspoon onion granules
¼ teaspoon ground black pepper

**1** Mix the ingredients in a small bowl.

## KEY
● RED MEAT
● PORK
● POULTRY
● SEAFOOD
● VEGETABLES

# MAKING MARINADES

**ACIDS**

citrus juices
tomatoes
vinegars
wine
yogurt

**OILS**

extra-virgin olive oil
rapeseed oil
toasted sesame oil

**GOOD FLAVOURS**

condiments          spices
finely chopped      zest of citrus fruit
vegetables
fresh or dried
herbs

In marinades you can add whatever you think might taste good, but before you start dumping ingredients into a bowl with all the restraint of a sailor on leave, let me give you some advice. Start with the basics. That means a little acidity, a good deal of oil, and a bunch of other good flavours. The ratio in a basic salad dressing is a good beginning. That's 1:3, or one part acidity to three parts oil. Then add your other flavours. The acidity will tenderize the food, especially the surface of the food, and the oil will provide moisture and richness, as well as carry other flavours. The other flavours, well, they just taste good.

If your marinade includes some acidic liquid, be sure to use a non-reactive container. This is a dish or bowl made of glass, plastic, stainless steel or china. A container made of aluminium, or some other metals, will react with acids and add a metallic flavour to food.

# MARINADES

## HOW LONG?

The right length of time varies, depending on the strength of the marinade and the food you are marinating. If your marinade includes intense ingredients like soy sauce, spirits, or hot chillies and strong spices, don't overdo it. A fish fillet should still taste like fish, not like a burning-hot, salt-soaked piece of protein. Also, if an acidic marinade is left too long on meat or fish, it can turn the surface dry or mushy. Here are some guidelines to get you going.

| TIME | TYPES OF FOOD |
|---|---|
| 15–30 minutes | Small foods, such as shellfish, fish fillets, cubed meat for kebabs, and tender vegetables |
| 1–3 hours | Thin cuts of boneless meat, such as chicken breasts, pork fillet, chops and steaks as well as sturdy vegetables |
| 2–6 hours | Thicker cuts of boneless or bone-in meat, such as leg of lamb, whole chickens and beef roasts |
| 6–12 hours | Big or tough cuts of meat, such as racks of ribs, whole hams, pork shoulders and turkeys |

## TANDOORI MARINADE

● ● ●

MAKES: about 475 ml/16 fl oz

350 ml/12 fl oz plain Greek yogurt
1 small onion, chopped
2 tablespoons chopped fresh ginger
2 tablespoons fresh lemon juice
2 tablespoons curry powder
2 tablespoons paprika
4 garlic cloves, roughly chopped
2 teaspoons sea salt
¼ teaspoon ground cayenne pepper

**1** Combine all of the ingredients in a food processor and process until smooth.

## LEMON MARINADE

● ● ●

MAKES: about 120 ml/4 fl oz

4 tablespoons extra-virgin olive oil
1 tablespoon grated lemon zest
3 tablespoons fresh lemon juice
1 tablespoon finely chopped garlic
1 teaspoon sea salt
½ teaspoon dried thyme

**1** Whisk all of the ingredients in a small bowl.

## SOUTHWEST MARINADE

● ● ● ●

MAKES: about 240 ml/8 fl oz

120 ml/4 fl oz fresh orange juice
3 tablespoons extra-virgin olive oil
2 tablespoons red wine vinegar
1 tablespoon finely chopped garlic
2 teaspoons chilli powder
1½ teaspoons dried oregano
1 teaspoon sea salt
½ teaspoon ground black pepper
½ teaspoon ground cinnamon

**1** Whisk all of the ingredients in a small bowl.

## WORCESTE-SHIRE PASTE

● ● ●

MAKES: about 5 tablespoons

2 tablespoons extra-virgin olive oil
2 tablespoons Worcestershire sauce
2 teaspoons cracked black pepper
2 teaspoons garlic granules
1½ teaspoons sea salt
1 teaspoon smoked paprika
1 teaspoon ground cumin
½ teaspoon ground cinnamon

**1** Whisk all of the ingredients in a small bowl.

## TARRAGON-CITRUS MARINADE

● ● ●

MAKES: about 240 ml/8 fl oz

4 tablespoons extra-virgin olive oil
4 tablespoons roughly chopped fresh
    tarragon leaves
Zest and juice of 1 orange
Zest and juice of 1 lemon
2 tablespoons sherry vinegar
2 teaspoons sea salt
1 teaspoon finely chopped garlic
1 teaspoon grated fresh ginger
½ teaspoon chilli seasoning
½ teaspoon ground black pepper

**1** Whisk all of the ingredients in a small bowl.

## WHOLEGRAIN MUSTARD MARINADE

● ● ● ●

MAKES: about 150 ml/5 fl oz

3 tablespoons wholegrain mustard
3 tablespoons extra-virgin olive oil
3 tablespoons red wine vinegar
2 teaspoons Worcestershire sauce
2 teaspoons finely chopped garlic
1 teaspoon dried thyme
½ teaspoon sea salt
½ teaspoon ground black pepper

**1** Whisk all of the ingredients in a small bowl.

# TERIYAKI MARINADE

● ● ● ● ●

MAKES: about 300 ml/½ pint

120 ml/4 fl oz pineapple juice
120 ml/4 fl oz soy sauce
4 tablespoons soft light brown sugar
2 tablespoons thinly sliced dark green
    spring onion tops
1 tablespoon grated fresh ginger
2 teaspoons finely chopped garlic

**1** Whisk all of the ingredients in a medium bowl, until the sugar dissolves.

# SWEET BOURBON MARINADE

● ●

MAKES: about 475 ml/16 fl oz

120 ml/4 fl oz bourbon
125 g/4 oz soft light brown sugar
5 tablespoons soy sauce
5 tablespoons fresh lemon juice
2 tablespoons Worcestershire sauce
2 teaspoons finely chopped garlic
2 teaspoons finely chopped thyme leaves

**1** Whisk all of the ingredients in a medium bowl.

# POMEGRANATE MARINADE

● ●

MAKES: about 350 ml/12 fl oz

3 tablespoons pomegranate molasses
3 tablespoons balsamic vinegar
2 teaspoons finely chopped thyme leaves
¾ teaspoon sea salt
½ teaspoon crushed red chilli flakes
240 ml/8 fl oz extra-virgin olive oil

**1** Whisk the molasses, vinegar, thyme, salt and chilli flakes in a medium bowl. Gradually whisk in the oil.

## KEY
● RED MEAT
● PORK
● POULTRY
● SEAFOOD
● VEGETABLES

# MAKING BRINES

## STEP 1

A well-balanced brine begins with 8–16 tablespoons of sea salt for each 4 litres/7 pints of water or other liquid.

## STEP 2

Whisk vigorously to dissolve the salt in cold water, and include any herbs and spices you like.

## STEP 3

Submerge all areas of the meat in the brine, cover the bowl with clingfilm, and refrigerate.

# BRINES

When it comes to making brines, the key is to use the right ratio of salt to water. Too much or too little salt can lead to major disappointments. Begin with 8–16 tablespoons of sea salt for each 4 litres/7 pints of water or other liquid. This level of saltiness creates a subtle background of flavour inside the meat. What happens is that the salt penetrates the meat and changes the structure of the protein so that the cells inside the meat are able to trap more moisture and flavour. Nature likes equilibrium, so the saltiness inside the meat rises until it is equal to the saltiness in the brine outside the meat. If you like, you can also add sugar to your brine, about the same amount as the salt, and the sugar will complement the saltiness and also caramelize nicely on the surface of the food. Then you can add whatever other flavours you like, including a variety of herbs and spices.

If your brine includes some acidic liquid, be sure to use a non-reactive container. This is a dish or bowl made of glass, plastic, stainless steel or china. A container made of aluminium, or some other metals, will react with acids and add a metallic flavour to food.

The most deserving candidates for brining are big, lean cuts of meat, such as pork loins and whole turkeys, which you should soak for several hours. But even small items like pork chops, chicken pieces and salmon fillets are bound to be juicier and more flavourful if you brine them for an hour or two.

Don't be deterred by the thought of always having to spend a long time boiling and cooling a brine, as many cookbooks suggest for dissolving the salt. Just use a light and flaky salt. All you need is a whisk to dissolve that type of salt in cold water.

Whatever you brine should be completely submerged, covered with clingfilm, and then refrigerated.

# ROSEMARY BRINE

MAKES: about 4 litres/7 pints

4 litres/7 pints water
125 g/4 oz sea salt
125 g/4 oz granulated sugar
2 tablespoons dried rosemary
1 tablespoon caraway seeds
1 tablespoon garlic granules
2 teaspoons ground black pepper

**1** Combine all of the ingredients in a large container. Whisk to dissolve the sugar and salt.

# BUTTERMILK BRINE

MAKES: about 750 ml/1¼ pints

475 ml/16 fl oz cold buttermilk
240 ml/8 fl oz water
8 tablespoons sea salt
1 tablespoon wholegrain mustard
1 tablespoon finely chopped tarragon leaves

**1** Whisk all of the ingredients in a medium bowl until the salt dissolves.

# BEER BRINE

MAKES: 2 litres/3½ pints

1 litre/1¾ pints lager
850 ml/1½ water
8 tablespoons sea salt
125 g/4 oz soft light brown sugar

**1** Combine all of the ingredients in a large container. Whisk to dissolve the sugar and salt.

# CIDER BRINE

MAKES: about 475 ml/16 fl oz

350 ml/12 fl oz cider
8 tablespoons sea salt
1 tablespoon dried rosemary
1 tablespoon dried sage
1½ teaspoons dried thyme
½ teaspoon black peppercorns

**1** Whisk all of the ingredients in a medium bowl until the salt dissolves.

# BOURBON BRINE

MAKES: about 475 ml/16 fl oz

120 ml/4 fl oz bourbon
120 ml/4 fl oz water
4 tablespoons soft light brown sugar
2 tablespoons sea salt
½ teaspoon crushed red chilli flakes
240 ml/8 fl oz ice cubes

**1** Combine the bourbon, water, brown sugar, salt and chilli flakes in a medium saucepan over a medium heat. Stir until the sugar and salt dissolve. Remove from the heat and stir in the ice cubes to cool the brine quickly.

# CHILLI BRINE

MAKES: about 1 litre/1¾ pints

1 litre/1¾ pints cold water
4 tablespoons sea salt
2 tablespoons granulated sugar
1½ teaspoons chilli powder
Zest of 1 lime

**1** Whisk all of the ingredients in a large bowl until the salt and sugar dissolve.

# APPLE BRINE

MAKES: about 2.2 litres/4 pints

2 litres/3½ pints chilled unsweetened apple juice
8 tablespoons sea salt
120 ml/4 fl oz soy sauce
75 g/3 oz fresh ginger, thinly sliced
1 tablespoon dried rosemary
1 teaspoon black peppercorns
Zest of 2 lemons, removed in wide strips with a vegetable peeler
2 bay leaves

1 Combine half the apple juice, the salt, soy sauce, ginger, rosemary, peppercorns, lemon zest strips and bay leaves in a medium saucepan over a medium heat and bring to a simmer to release the flavours, stirring occasionally. Pour into a large heatproof bowl set in a larger bowl of iced water. Leave to stand for about 30 minutes, until chilled, stirring often. Stir the remaining chilled apple juice into the brine.

# SPICY GARLIC BRINE

MAKES: about 1.5 litres/2¾ pints

1.5 litres/2¾ pints cold water
5 tablespoons sea salt
4 tablespoons granulated sugar
2 garlic cloves, peeled and crushed
4 whole allspice berries, crushed
4 whole cloves, crushed
1 bay leaf, broken in half
1 teaspoon dried marjoram

1 Combine the water, salt and sugar in a large bowl. Whisk until the salt and sugar dissolve. Add the remaining ingredients.

# HONEY AND HERB BRINE

MAKES: about 2 litres/3½ pints

2 litres/3½ pints water
8 tablespoons sea salt
225 g/8 oz runny honey
2 teaspoons dried rosemary
2 teaspoons dried sage
1½ teaspoons dried marjoram
1 teaspoon black peppercorns
2 bay leaves

1 Whisk all of the ingredients in a large container until the salt dissolves.

# CRANBERRY-ORANGE BRINE

MAKES: about 5 litres/8¾ pints

2 litres/3½ pints cranberry juice
2 litres/3½ pints fresh orange juice
2 small garlic heads, cloves crushed but not peeled
150 g/5 oz sea salt
4 tablespoons crushed red chilli flakes
4 tablespoons fennel seeds
125 g/4 oz fresh ginger, thinly sliced
6 bay leaves
1 litre/1¾ pints ice cubes

1 Combine all the ingredients, except the ice, in a large, non-reactive pan over a high heat and bring to the boil. Boil for about 1 minute and then remove from the heat. Add the ice cubes and leave for about 1½ hours to cool to room temperature.

KEY
● RED MEAT
● PORK
● POULTRY
● SEAFOOD
● VEGETABLES

# MAKING SAUCES

## SWEET

black treacle
brown sugar
granulated sugar
hoisin sauce
honey

ketchup
maple syrup
soft drinks

## SOUR

balsamic vinegar
cider vinegar
fresh lemon or
lime juice
juice from a pickle
or relish jar

mustard
red or white wine
vinegar
rice vinegar

## SPICY

black pepper
cayenne pepper
crushed red chilli flakes
fresh or dried chillies
horseradish
hot pepper sauces

## SALTY

anchovies
fish sauce
olives
sea salt
soy sauce

Worcestershire
sauce

# SAUCES

If you had to pick just one way to give your food a special edge that reflects your taste, think sauces, but proceed with caution. Sauces represent a giant playground of creativity and, as with marinades, there are almost limitless possibilities, so it's easy to go a little crazy. I suggest starting with a basic barbecue sauce and aiming for a nice blend of sweetness, sourness, spiciness and saltiness. One way to do this is to choose one or two ingredients from each category on this page. The most traditional barbecue sauces are based on tomato ketchup, for sweetness and thickness, and some version of vinegar, for sourness. After that you can add whatever sources of spiciness and saltiness you prefer. But don't forget that little something extra that really sets a great sauce apart. Let's call it the 'extra factor'. It could be almost anything. Here are some options to consider.

THE 'EXTRA' FACTOR:
**any spice imaginable**
**liquid smoke**
**spirits**
**wine**
**tomato sauce**
**fruit preserves**
**butter or extra-virgin olive oil**
**chicken or beef stock**
**coffee**
**you name it …**

# RED WINE SAUCE

MAKES: about 180 ml/6 fl oz

350 ml/12 fl oz dry red wine
1 finely chopped shallot
1 tablespoon tomato purée
2 teaspoons balsamic vinegar
½ teaspoon Worcestershire sauce
40 g/1½ oz unsalted butter, cut into
    3 pieces
Sea salt
Ground black pepper

**1** Bring the wine and shallot to the boil in a small saucepan over a high heat. Then immediately reduce the heat to medium and simmer for 15 to 20 minutes until the wine has reduced to about a third. Add the tomato purée, vinegar and Worcestershire sauce. Remove from the heat and add the butter piece by piece, whisking to incorporate the butter into the sauce. Season with salt and pepper.

# CREAMY MUSTARD SAUCE

MAKES: about 180ml/6 fl oz

15 g/½ oz unsalted butter
1 finely chopped shallot
120 ml/4 fl oz beef stock
180 ml/6 fl oz whipping cream
3 tablespoons wholegrain mustard
Sea salt

**1** Melt the butter in a medium frying pan over a medium heat. Add the shallot and cook for 1 to 2 minutes until softened, stirring often. Add the stock and bring to the boil over a high heat. Cook for 2 to 3 minutes until the stock reduces by half. Add the cream and bring to a simmer (do not boil). Whisk in the mustard and simmer for 3 to 5 minutes until the sauce is reduced to 180 ml/6 fl oz and is thick enough to coat the back of a spoon. Season with salt.

# TOMATO-CHIMICHURRI SAUCE

MAKES: about 240 ml/8 fl oz

50 g/2 oz flat-leaf parsley
120 ml/4 fl oz extra-virgin olive oil
15 g/½ oz fresh coriander
4 tablespoons oil-packed sun-dried
    tomatoes, drained
3 garlic cloves
¾ teaspoon crushed red chilli flakes
Sea salt
Ground black pepper

**1** Combine all the ingredients except the salt and black pepper in a food processor. Pulse until you get a semi-smooth consistency. Season with salt and pepper.

# THREE-HERB HAZELNUT PESTO

MAKES: about 400 ml/14 fl oz

25 g/1 oz fresh coriander
25 g/1 oz flat-leaf parsley
15 g/½ oz oregano
4 tablespoons hazelnuts, toasted and
    skins removed
4 tablespoons sherry vinegar
3–5 garlic cloves, roughly chopped
½ teaspoon crushed red chilli flakes
120 ml/4 fl oz extra-virgin olive oil
Sea salt
Ground black pepper

**1** Process the fresh herbs, hazelnuts, vinegar, garlic and chilli flakes in a food processor. Then, with the motor running, slowly add the oil to make a thin paste. Season with salt and pepper.

# RED CHILLI BARBECUE SAUCE

MAKES: about 475 ml/16 fl oz

4 dried chillies, about 20 g/¾ oz total
    weight, stems removed
2 tablespoons rapeseed oil
240 ml/8 fl oz hot water
120 ml/4 fl oz tomato ketchup
3 tablespoons soy sauce
2 tablespoons balsamic vinegar
3 garlic cloves, crushed
1 teaspoon ground cumin
½ teaspoon dried oregano
¼ teaspoon sea salt
¼ teaspoon ground black pepper

**1** Cut the chillies crossways into sections about 5 cm/2 inches long. Remove most of the seeds. Warm the oil in a medium frying pan over a high heat. Add the chillies and toast them for 2 to 3 minutes, turning once, until they puff up and begin to change colour. Transfer the chillies and oil to a small bowl. Cover with the hot water and soak for 30 minutes. Pour the chillies, along with the oil and water, into a blender or food processor. Add the remaining ingredients and process until very smooth.

## KEY
● RED MEAT
● PORK
● POULTRY
● SEAFOOD
● VEGETABLES

# TOP TEN SMOKING TIPS

## 1 START EARLY.
Many of the flavour compounds in smoke are fat and water soluble, which means that whatever you are cooking will absorb smoky flavours best when it is raw. As the surface cooks and dries out, the smoke does not penetrate as well.

## 2 GO LOW AND SLOW (MOST OF THE TIME).
Real barbecue is cooked slowly over low, indirect heat/roasting – with wood smoke – because that's a traditional way to make sinewy meats so moist and tender that you hardly need teeth. But don't miss easy opportunities for adding sweet wood aromas to foods that are grilled over a hot fire for just minutes, like steaks, prawns, and even vegetables.

## 3 REGULATE THE HEAT WITH A WATER PAN.
Big fluctuations in smoking temperatures can tighten and dry out foods. Whenever you cook for longer than an hour with charcoal, use a pan of water to help stabilize the heat and add some humidity. Obviously a water smoker already has one, but for a charcoal grill, use a large disposable foil tray, and don't forget to refill it.

## 4 DON'T OVERDO IT.
The biggest mistake rookies make is adding too much wood, chunk after chunk, to the point where the food tastes bitter. In general, you should smoke food for no longer than half its cooking time. Also, the smoke should flow like a gentle stream, not as if it is billowing out of a steam engine.

## 5 WHITE SMOKE IS GOOD; BLACK SMOKE IS BAD.
Clean streams of whitish smoke can layer your food with the intoxicating scents of smouldering wood. But if your fire lacks enough ventilation, or your food is directly over the fire and the juices are burning, blackish smoke can taint your food or lead to unpleasant surprises when you lift the lid.

## 6

### KEEP THE AIR MOVING.
Keep the vents on your charcoal grill open, and position the vent on the lid on the side opposite the coals. The open vents will draw smoke from the charcoal and wood below so that it swirls over your food and out of the top properly, giving you the best ventilation and the cleanest smoke. If the fire gets too hot, close the top vent almost all the way.

## 7

### DON'T GO GOLFING.
Smoking is a relatively low-maintenance way of cooking – but remain mindful and be safe. Never leave a lit fire unattended, and check the temperature every hour or so. You might need to adjust the vents or add more charcoal.

## 8

### TRY NOT TO PEEK.
Every time you open a grill, you lose heat and smoke – two of the most important elements for making a great meal. Open the lid only when you really need to tend to the fire, the water pan or the food. Ideally take care of them all at once – and quickly. Otherwise, relax and keep a lid on it.

## 9

### LET THE BARK GET DARK.
When smoked properly, ribs and large chunks of beef and pork should be enveloped in a dark mahogany, borderline black crust called 'bark'. This bark is the consequence of fat and spices sizzling with smoke on the surface of the meat developing into a caramelized crust. So before you take your dinner off the grill or wrap it in foil, make sure you've waited long enough for the delicious, dark bark to develop.

## 10

### FEATURE THE STAR ATTRACTION.
The main ingredient in any smoked recipe is like the lead singer in a rock-and-roll band. Every other flavour should play a supporting role. In other words, don't upstage something inherently delicious with a potent marinade, heavy-handed seasonings or thick coats of sauce. Harmonizing flavours in ways that feature the main ingredient is what separates the masters from the masses.

# Recipes

Now that you have a well-stocked store cupboard plus the necessary tools and equipment, practice your skills by preparing the grill and take your pick of the recipes that follow. Recipes are grouped into starters, red meat, pork, poultry and seafood as well as vegetable and side dishes to accompany them. Don't forget to refer back to the smoking basics whenever you need to.

# Starters

# HICKORY SPICED MIXED NUTS

1 teaspoon soft light brown sugar

1 teaspoon ground cumin

¼ teaspoon ground cayenne pepper

500 g/1 lb salted mixed nuts *or*
    peanuts

2 teaspoons groundnut oil

1 large handful hickory wood chips,
    soaked in water for at least
    30 minutes

*Use a tray that is large enough to spread all the nuts in a single layer so they are all exposed to smoke.*

1 Prepare a two-zone fire for medium heat (180–230°C/350–450°F) (see pages 20–21).

2 Mix the brown sugar, cumin and cayenne pepper in a large disposable foil tray. Add the nuts and stir. Add the groundnut oil, toss to coat and set aside.

3 Brush the cooking grate clean. Drain and add the wood chips to the charcoal and put the lid on the grill. When the wood begins to smoke, roast the nuts over **INDIRECT MEDIUM HEAT** for about 20 minutes, with the lid closed, until they turn a shade or two darker and have developed a good smoky flavour. Wearing insulated barbecue mitts or oven gloves, remove the pan from the grill and leave the nuts in the pan to cool completely. They will crisp as they cool.

4 Serve at room temperature. Store any remaining nuts in an airtight container.

# SMOKED FISH SPREAD
## WITH GOAT'S CHEESE AND BRANDY

**IDEAL GRILL:**

**SMOKE INTENSITY:** moderate

**PREP TIME:** 30 minutes

**COOKING TIME:** about 18 minutes

**COOLING TIME:** 20 minutes

**CHILLING TIME:** at least 2 hours

**SERVES:** 12

1 trout *or* salmon fillet (with skin),
    about 500 g/1 lb
2 tablespoons extra-virgin olive oil
Sea salt

1 large handful apple wood chips,
    soaked in water for at least 30
    minutes

225 g/8 oz goats' cheese, at room
    temperature
50 g/2 oz unsalted butter, softened
4 tablespoons fresh lemon juice
2 tablespoons brandy
1  shallot, finely chopped
½ teaspoon ground black pepper
⅛ teaspoon hot pepper sauce

1 tablespoon finely chopped chives
    or flat-leaf parsley
Sliced rye bread, toasted
Wholegrain Dijon mustard

*The fish can be smoked, stored
in an airtight container and
refrigerated for 1 day.*

**1** Prepare a two-zone fire for medium-low heat (about 180°C/350°F) (see pages 18–19).

**2** Brush the fish on both sides with the oil and season the flesh evenly with ½ teaspoon salt.

**3** Brush the cooking grate clean. Drain and add the wood chips to the charcoal and put the lid on the grill. When the wood begins to smoke, cook the fish, flesh side down first, over **GRILLING/DIRECT MEDIUM-LOW HEAT** for 3 minutes, with the lid closed. Turn the fish, flesh side up, and move it over **ROASTING/INDIRECT MEDIUM-LOW HEAT**. Close the lid and cook for about 15 minutes until the flesh is opaque in the centre. Remove from the grill and leave to cool for 20 minutes.

**4** Remove and discard the skin from the fish and cut the flesh into chunks. Place the chunks in a food processor fitted with a chopping blade. Add the cheese, butter, lemon juice, brandy, shallots, pepper and hot pepper sauce. Process until smooth, scraping down the sides of the bowl once or twice. Season with salt. Transfer the spread to a bowl, cover and refrigerate at least 2 hours until chilled.

**5** Just before serving, top with the chives. Serve chilled, with toasted rye bread and mustard.

*After processing the smoked fish with the cheese and other ingredients, be sure to chill the spread for at least 2 hours so that stronger flavours have time to meld with the subtler ones, creating a well-balanced overall taste.*

# TROUT AND ARTICHOKE DIP

**IDEAL GRILL:**

**SMOKE INTENSITY:** moderate

**PREP TIME:** 30 minutes

**COOKING TIME:** about 10 minutes

**COOLING TIME:** 1 hour

**CHILLING TIME:** at least 1 hour

**SPECIAL EQUIPMENT:** fish slice

**SERVINGS:** 8–12

2 whole trout, each about
    250 g/8 oz, butterflied, not
    boned, heads removed
Rapeseed oil
Sea salt
Ground black pepper

2 large handfuls mesquite wood
    chips, soaked in water for at least
    30 minutes

400-g/14-oz artichoke hearts
    packed in water
120 ml/4 fl oz cup mayonnaise
4 tablespoons soured cream
2 tablespoons dill, finely chopped
1 shallot, finely chopped
Finely grated zest of 1 lemon
1 tablespoon fresh lemon juice
1 tablespoon white wine vinegar
½ teaspoon dried oregano
Hot pepper sauce
Crackers or crisp rye flat bread

1 Prepare a two-zone fire for medium heat (180–230°C/350–450°F) (see pages 20–21).

2 Brush the skin of the trout with oil and season the flesh lightly with salt and pepper.

3 Brush the cooking grate clean. Drain and add the wood chips to the charcoal and put the lid on the grill. When the wood begins to smoke, place the trout, opened and skin side down, over **ROASTING/INDIRECT MEDIUM HEAT**. Close the bottom vents, cover the grill and cook for about 10 minutes, until the flesh flakes when pierced with the tip of a knife. Using a fish slice, transfer the trout to a chopping board and leave for about 1 hour to cool to room temperature.

4 Starting at the head end, lift and remove the backbone and any attached bones. Using a paring knife, remove any stray bones. Peel the skin off the flesh. Discard the skin and bones.

5 Drain the artichoke hearts in a fine sieve and rinse under cold water. Squeeze the excess water from the artichokes. Pulse the artichokes in a food processor until roughly chopped. Transfer to a serving bowl and gently mix in the trout, mayonnaise, soured cream, dill, shallots, lemon zest and juice, vinegar and oregano. Season with salt and hot pepper sauce. Cover and refrigerate for at least 1 hour, until chilled. (The dip can be refrigerated for up to 3 days.) Serve chilled with crackers.

*The cooked trout cannot be picked up with tongs – it will fall apart. And a standard slice is simply too small. Use a wide, large fish slice to get the trout off the cooking grate and on to your chopping board.*

# CEDAR-PLANKED BRIE
## WITH CHERRY CHUTNEY AND TOASTED ALMONDS

IDEAL
GRILL:

SMOKE INTENSITY: moderate

PREP TIME: 20 minutes

COOKING TIME: about 10 minutes

SPECIAL EQUIPMENT: 1 untreated
cedar plank, 30–37 cm/
12–15 inches long and about
18 cm/7 inches wide and
1–1.5 cm/½–¾ inch thick, soaked
in water for at least 1 hour

SERVES: 4–6

### CHUTNEY
2 teaspoons vegetable oil
½ small onion, finely chopped
½ teaspoon garlic, finely chopped
2 teaspoons peeled, fresh ginger,
    finely chopped
150 g/5 oz cherry jam
Ground cinnamon
Crushed red chilli flakes

250 g/8 oz wheel of Brie cheese
4 tablespoons flaked almonds,
    toasted
Baguette slices or crackers

*To toast the almonds, spread
them on a baking sheet and
bake for about 10 minutes in
a preheated 180°C/350°F/
Gas mark 4 oven until golden
brown and fragrant, stirring
occasionally. Transfer to a plate
to cool.*

*The cheese should be cool, no more than 10 minutes out of the refrigerator. If it's
too warm, it will break and run all over the grill. Also, do not use overripe Brie, a
wheel that is collapsing at its centre. It, too, will break and run all over the grill.*

1 Warm the oil in a small, heavy saucepan over a medium heat. Add the onion and
cook for about 5 minutes, stirring often, until golden. Add the garlic and stir for
about 30 seconds until fragrant. Stir in the ginger, jam, a pinch of cinnamon and a
pinch of chilli flakes and bring to a simmer. Reduce the heat to very low and cook
for 3 minutes. Transfer to a bowl to cool.

2 Prepare a two-zone fire for medium heat (180–230°C/350–450°F) (see pages
20–21).

3 Brush the cooking grate clean. Place the soaked plank over **GRILLING/DIRECT
MEDIUM HEAT** and close the lid. After 5–10 minutes, when the plank begins to
smoke, you are ready to introduce the Brie.

4 Set the Brie in the centre of the plank and cook over **GRILLING/DIRECT MEDIUM
HEAT** for about 10 minutes, with the lid closed, until the cheese softens and
the rind turns a pale golden brown. Use a wide spatula to transfer the Brie to a
serving plate.

5 Spoon half the chutney over the cheese and top with the toasted almonds. Serve
with bread or crackers and the remaining chutney on the side.

# CHILE CON QUESO

**IDEAL**
**GRILL:**

**SMOKE INTENSITY:** strong

**PREP TIME:** 15 minutes

**COOKING TIME:** 30 60 minutes
to 1 hour

**SPECIAL EQUIPMENT:**
25–30-cm/10–12-inch cast-iron
frying pan

**SERVES:** 8–10

350-g/12-oz block mild Cheddar
    cheese
350-g/12-oz block mature Cheddar
    cheese

4 mesquite wood chunks

## SALSA
1 tablespoon extra-virgin olive oil
1 onion, chopped
1 jalapeño chilli, deseeded and finely
    chopped
1 large garlic clove, finely chopped
3 ripe plum tomatoes, deseeded and
    chopped
2 teaspoons dried oregano
Sea salt

1 tablespoon finely chopped fresh
    coriander
350 g/12 oz tortilla chips

1 Prepare the smoker for roasting/indirect cooking with extremely low heat (about 80°C/175°F) (see pages 23–25).

2 Place the blocks of cheese side by side, about 5 cm/2 inches apart, in a 10–12-inch/25–30-cm cast-iron frying pan.

3 Brush the cooking grate clean. Add the wood chunks to the charcoal and put the lid on the smoker. When smoke appears, place the frying pan over **ROASTING/INDIRECT EXTREMELY LOW HEAT**, close the lid, and cook for 30–60 minutes until the cheese has melted into two pools that run together. Do not overcook or the cheese may separate.

4 Meanwhile, heat the oil in a medium frying pan over a medium heat. Add the onion, chilli and garlic and cook for about 3 minutes until the onion softens, stirring occasionally. Add the tomatoes and oregano and cook for about 5 minutes, stirring occasionally, until the tomatoes give off their juices. Remove from the heat and season with salt.

5 Spoon the salsa over the melted cheese in the frying pan and sprinkle with the coriander. Serve warm with tortilla chips.

*To turn the chilli con queso into a main course, add a can of black or pinto beans, drained and rinsed, to the pan with the tomatoes. Serve with warm flour tortillas, shredded lettuce and thin red onion slices.*

# BARBECUED OYSTERS
## WITH TOMATO-HORSERADISH SAUCE

**IDEAL GRILL:**

**SMOKE INTENSITY:** moderate

**PREP TIME:** 15 minutes, plus about 30 minutes to shuck the oysters

**COOKING TIME:** 2–4 minutes

**SPECIAL EQUIPMENT:** oyster knife

**SERVES:** 4

*If you don't have an oyster knife, there is a common kitchen utensil that will also do the job – an old-fashioned bottle opener, the kind that has one pointed end and one blunt end. Wedge the pointed end, with the point facing up, into the small opening in the shell hinge. Holding the oyster secure with one hand, use the other hand to press down on the opener handle to act as a lever to prise the oyster shells apart. Use a paring knife to cut and loosen the oyster body from the shells.*

### SAUCE
2 teaspoons rapeseed oil
1 spring onion (white part only), finely chopped (reserve the green part)
2 tablespoons finely chopped celery
1 small garlic clove, finely chopped
240 ml/8 fl oz tomato sauce
1 tablespoon fresh lemon juice
½ teaspoon Worcestershire sauce
1 teaspoon horseradish sauce
1 teaspoon soft light brown sugar
Hot pepper sauce

2 dozen large, fresh oysters
1 large handful cherry wood chips, soaked in water for at least 30 minutes

1 Heat the oil In a small saucepan over a medium heat. Add the spring onion (white part), celery and garlic and cook for about 2 minutes, stirring occasionally, until the celery softens. Add the tomato sauce, lemon juice, Worcestershire sauce, horseradish and brown sugar and bring to a simmer. Reduce the heat to medium-low and simmer, uncovered, for about 5 minutes, stirring occasionally, to blend the flavours. Remove from the heat. Season with hot pepper sauce.

2 Shuck the oysters: Grip each oyster, flat side up, in a folded tea towel. Find the small opening between the shells near the hinge and prise it open with an oyster knife. Try not to spill the delicious juices, known as the 'oyster liquor', in the bottom of the shell. Cut the oyster meat loose from the top shell and then loosen the oyster from the bottom shell by running the oyster knife carefully under the body. Discard the top, flatter shell.

3 Prepare a two-zone fire for high heat (230–290°C/450–550°F) (see pages 18–19).

4 Spoon a generous teaspoon of the sauce on each oyster. Reserve the remaining sauce.

5 Brush the cooking grates clean. Drain and add the wood chips to the charcoal and put the lid on the grill. When the wood begins to smoke, cook the oysters, shell side down, over **GRILLING/DIRECT HIGH HEAT** for 2–4 minutes, with the lid closed, until the sauce and oyster juices start to bubble and the edges of the oyster meat curl. Using tongs, carefully remove the oysters from the grill. Finely chop the reserved green part of the spring onion and scatter on top of the oysters. Serve with the remaining sauce.

# SMOKED CHICKEN DRUMETTES
## WITH ORANGE-HONEY GLAZE

**IDEAL GRILL:**

**SMOKE INTENSITY:** strong

**PREP TIME:** 15 minutes

**COOKING TIME:** 20–30 minutes

**SERVES:** 6–8

20 chicken drumsticks, about 1.5
    kg/3 lb total weight
1 teaspoon Sea salt
½ teaspoon ground black pepper

### GLAZE
150 g/5 oz orange marmalade
4 tablespoons runny honey
1 teaspoon Sea salt
1 teaspoon garlic granules
1 teaspoon onion granules
½ teaspoon ground cayenne pepper

2 large handfuls hickory wood chips,
    soaked in water for at least 30
    minutes

**1** Season the drumsticks evenly with the salt and pepper.

**2** Prepare a two-zone fire for medium heat (180-230°C/350-450°F) (see pages 18-19).

**3** Combine the glaze ingredients in a small, heavy saucepan over a medium heat and stir for 5-6 minutes until the marmalade melts. Remove from the heat and cover to keep warm.

**4** Brush the cooking grate clean. Drain and add the wood chips to the charcoal and put the lid on the grill. When the wood begins to smoke, cook the drumsticks over **ROASTING/INDIRECT MEDIUM HEAT** for 20-30 minutes with the lid closed as much as possible, until the juices run clear and the meat is no longer pink at the bone, turning and basting with the glaze two or three times during the final 10-12 minutes. Remove from the grill and serve warm.

*Cooking the drumsticks over indirect heat breaks down some of the chewy characteristics of the meat.*

# Red Meat

# MESQUITE-GRILLED CHEESEBURGERS
## WITH WARM CHIPOTLE SALSA

**IDEAL GRILL:**

**SMOKE INTENSITY:** strong

**PREP TIME:** 20 minutes

**COOKING TIME:** 20–22 minutes

**SERVES:** 4

750 g/1½ lb minced beef (80% lean)

2 teaspoons ground cumin

1½ teaspoons ground black pepper

Sea salt

2 tablespoons extra-virgin olive oil

1 small red onion, finely chopped

1 garlic clove, finely chopped

4 plum tomatoes, each cut in half
    lengthways

2 large handfuls mesquite wood
    chips, soaked in water for at least
    30 minutes

3 tablespoons finely chopped fresh
    coriander

100 ml/3½ fl oz chilli sauce

1 tablespoon fresh lime juice

1 red pepper, finely chopped

4 slices smoked Cheddar or smoked
    Gouda cheese, each about
    25 g/1 oz

4 hamburger buns

*For spicier salsa, add adobo
sauce from the canned chipotle
chillies to taste.*

**1** Gently combine the mince, cumin, pepper and 1½ teaspoons salt in a large bowl. Shape into four burgers of equal size, each about 1.5 cm/¾ inch thick. With your thumb or the back of a spoon, make a shallow indentation about 2.5 cm/1 inch wide in the centre of each burger. This will help the burgers cook evenly and prevent them from puffing on the grill. Cover and refrigerate until ready to cook.

**2** Prepare a two-zone fire for high heat (230–290°C/450–550°F) (see pages 20–21).

**3** Warm 1 tablespoon of the oil in a medium frying pan over a medium heat. Add the onion and garlic and cook for about 3 minutes, stirring occasionally, until the onion is tender. Transfer to a medium bowl. Brush the tomatoes with the remaining 1 tablespoon of oil.

**4** Brush the cooking grate clean. Drain and add half of the wood chips to the charcoal and put the lid on the grill. When smoke appears, place the tomato halves, cut side up, over **ROASTING/INDIRECT HIGH HEAT**. Close the lid and cook for about 12 minutes until the tomato juices are bubbling and the skins split. Remove from the grill. Remove and discard the tomato skins and roughly chop the tomatoes. Add the tomatoes, coriander, red pepper, chilli and lime juice to the onion mixture. Season with salt. Set aside.

**5** Drain and add the remaining wood chips to the charcoal and put the lid on the grill. When the wood starts to smoke, cook the burgers over **GRILLING/DIRECT HIGH HEAT** for 8–10 minutes with the lid closed as much as possible, turning once, until cooked to medium doneness. During the last minute of cooking time, place a slice of cheese on each burger to melt and toast the burger buns, cut side down. Remove from the grill and build each burger with the salsa. Serve warm.

# LAMB CHEESEBURGERS
## WITH MANCHEGO AND HARISSA

IDEAL
GRILL:

SMOKE INTENSITY: moderate

PREP TIME: 30 minutes

SOAKING TIME: 20 minutes

COOKING TIME: 8–10 minutes

SERVES: 6

### HARISSA

40 g/1½ oz dried large dried chillies,
  stems, seeds and ribs removed
180 ml/6 fl oz boiling water
2 garlic cloves, roughly chopped
1½ tablespoons extra-virgin olive oil
1 tablespoon fresh lemon juice
½ teaspoon sea salt
¼ teaspoon caraway seeds
¼ teaspoon cumin seeds
¼ teaspoon coriander seeds

### BURGERS

1 kg/2 lb minced lamb
25 g/1 oz fresh coriander, finely
  chopped
2 teaspoons ground cumin
1½ teaspoons sea salt
¾ teaspoon ground black pepper

1 large handful oak wood chips,
  soaked in water for at least
  30 minutes
6 slices Manchego cheese, each
  about 25 g/1 oz
6 pitta breads, tops cut off
1 large tomato, cut into 6 slices
6 leaves green lettuce
6 slices red onion

*Look for dried chillies that are pliable and fragrant.*

1 Heat a large, heavy frying pan over a medium heat. Add the chillies, a few at a time, and cook until they turn a shade darker, about 20 seconds per side, using a wide metal spatula to press the chillies against the pan. Transfer to a heatproof bowl and leave to cool slightly. Roughly tear the chillies into 7-cm/3-inch pieces. Add enough of the boiling water to cover the chillies and let them soak for about 20 minutes until softened.

2 Drain the chillies, reserving the soaking liquid. Puree the chillies, garlic, oil, lemon juice, salt, caraway, cumin and coriander seeds in a blender, and add enough of the soaking liquid as needed to make a smooth paste.

3 Prepare a two-zone fire for high heat (230–290°C/450–550°F) (see pages 20–21).

4 Gently combine the burger ingredients in a large bowl and shape into six burgers of equal size, each about 1.5 cm/¾ inch thick. With your thumb or the back of a spoon, make a shallow indentation about 2.5/1 inch wide in the centre of each burger. This will help the burgers cook evenly and prevent them from puffing on the grill.

5 Brush the cooking grate clean. Drain and add the wood chips to the charcoal and put the lid on the grill. When smoke appears, cook the burgers over **GRILLING/ DIRECT HIGH HEAT** for 8–10 minutes with the lid closed as much as possible, turning them once when the burgers release easily from the grate without sticking, until cooked to medium doneness. During the last minute of cooking time, place a slice of cheese on each burger to melt and toast the pitta breads. Serve each burger in a pitta with a tomato slice, lettuce leaf, onion slice and some harissa.

# THREE-MEAT MEAT LOAF
## WITH ROASTED PEPPER GLAZE

**IDEAL GRILL:**

**SMOKE INTENSITY:** strong

**PREP TIME:** 40 minutes

**COOKING TIME:** 1–1¼ hours

**SPECIAL EQUIPMENT:** large disposable roasting tray, instant-read meat thermometer

**SERVES:** 6–8

### GLAZE
2 red peppers, about 300 g/10 oz total
240 ml/8 fl oz ketchup

### MEAT LOAF
1 tablespoon extra-virgin olive oil
1 onion, about 300 g/10 oz, finely chopped
2 poblano chillies, about 250 g/8 oz total weight, finely chopped
1 teaspoon finely chopped garlic
175 g/6 oz plain dried breadcrumbs
1 large egg, beaten
3 tablespoons Worcestershire sauce
2 teaspoons sea salt
1 teaspoon ground black pepper
750 g/1½ lb minced beef (85% lean)
250 g/8 oz minced pork
250 g/8 oz minced veal

2 large handfuls mesquite wood chips, soaked in water for at least 30 minutes

*Use a disposable roasting tray, as smoke will discolour a solid metal tin.*

1 Prepare a two-zone fire for medium heat (180–230°C/350–450°F) (see pages 20–21).

2 Brush the cooking grate clean. Grill the peppers over **GRILLING/DIRECT MEDIUM HEAT** for 10–12 minutes with the lid closed as much as possible, and turning occasionally, until blackened and blistered all over. Place the peppers in a bowl and cover with clingfilm to trap the steam. Leave to stand for about 10 minutes. Remove and discard the charred skin, stalks and seeds.

3 Purée the peppers until smooth in a blender or food processor. Add the ketchup and whirl until combined. Transfer to a bowl. Reserve 120 ml/4 fl oz of the glaze to use in the meat loaf.

4 Heat the oil in a large frying pan over a medium heat. Add the onion, chillies and garlic and cook for about 5 minutes, stirring occasionally, until the onion is tender. Transfer the mixture to a large bowl and leave to cool. Add the reserved glaze, the breadcrumbs, egg, Worcestershire sauce, salt and pepper to the onion mixture and stir to combine. Add the minced beef, pork and veal. Using your hands, gently combine the meat loaf ingredients until well blended.

5 Divide the meat loaf mixture in half and form into two loaves, each about 10 cm/4 inches wide by 15–18 cm/6–7 inches long. Place the loaves in a large disposable foil tray.

6 At this point, check the temperature of the grill. If necessary, add enough lit or unlit briquettes to the charcoal to raise the temperature of the grill to 180–230°C/350–450°F. If using unlit briquettes, leave the grill lid off to help them light faster.

7 Drain and add one handful of the wood chips to the charcoal and put the lid on the grill. When the wood begins to smoke, cook the meat loaves in the tray over **ROASTING/INDIRECT MEDIUM HEAT** for 30 minutes with the lid closed. Brush the top of the loaves with 4 tablespoons of the glaze. Drain and add the remaining wood chips to the charcoal. Continue cooking for 20–30 minutes more, rotating the pan once, until an instant-read meat thermometer inserted in the centre of each loaf registers 74°C/165°F. Carefully transfer the tray to a heatproof surface and leave to rest for about 10 minutes.

8 Remove the loaves from the tray and cut into 1 cm/½-inch slices. Serve warm with the remaining glaze.

# MESQUITE SKIRT STEAK
## WITH SALPICÓN SALAD

**IDEAL GRILL:**

**SMOKE INTENSITY:** moderate

**PREP TIME:** 30 minutes

**COOKING TIME:** 12–16 minutes

**SERVES:** 4

## PASTE
2 tablespoons extra-virgin olive oil
2 tablespoons fresh lime juice
2 tablespoons chilli powder
2 teaspoons ground cumin
1 teaspoon finely chopped garlic
1 teaspoon sea salt

875 g/1¾ lb skirt steak, 1–1.5 cm/
½–¾ inch thick, trimmed of excess
surface fat, cut into 30-cm/12-
inch pieces

## SALAD
500 g/1 lb very small red-skinned
potatoes, scrubbed
2 cobs fresh corn, outer leaves and
silk removed
1 ripe avocado, chopped
4 radishes, thinly sliced
2 spring onions (white and light
green parts only), thinly sliced
4 tablespoons finely chopped fresh
coriander
2 tablespoons fresh lime juice
1 canned chipotle chilli in adobo
sauce, finely chopped
1 garlic clove, finely chopped
120 ml/4 fl oz extra-virgin olive oil
Sea salt
Ground black pepper

1 large handful mesquite wood chips,
soaked in water for at least
30 minutes

Flour tortillas (15 cm/6 inches)
(optional)

*Skirt steak is typically well marbled with fat, which means it can be quite juicy and rich, but it can be chewy when it is undercooked, so cook until at least medium rare.*

1 Whisk the paste ingredients in a small bowl. Spread the paste on both sides of each steak. Set aside at room temperature for 15–30 minutes before cooking.

2 Put the potatoes in a medium saucepan and add salted water to cover. Bring to the boil over high heat. Reduce the heat to medium and cook the potatoes for about 20 minutes until tender when pierced with the tip of a knife. Drain, rinse under cold water and drain again. Cut each potato in half, transfer to a medium bowl and refrigerate to cool.

3 Prepare a two-zone fire for high heat (230–290°C/450–550°F) (see pages 20–21).

4 Brush the cooking grate clean. Cook the corn over **GRILLING/DIRECT HIGH HEAT** for 8–10 minutes, with the lid closed as much as possible, turning often, until the kernels are brown in spots all over. Remove from the grill and set aside. When the corn is cool enough to handle, cut the kernels from the cobs. Add to the bowl with the potatoes along with the avocado, radishes, spring onions and coriander.

5 Whisk the lime juice, chilli and garlic in a small bowl. Gradually whisk in the oil. Pour over the potato mixture and toss to combine. Season with salt and pepper. Refrigerate while cooking the steaks.

6 Drain and add the wood chips to the charcoal and put the lid on the grill. When smoke appears, cook the steaks over **GRILLING/DIRECT HIGH HEAT** with the lid closed as much as possible and turning once or twice, until cooked to your desired doneness, 4–6 minutes for medium rare (if flare-ups occur, move the steaks temporarily over roasting/indirect heat). Remove from the grill and leave to rest for 3–5 minutes.

7 Cut the steaks across the grain into 1 cm/½-inch slices. Serve immediately with the salad and warm tortillas, if liked.

# SMOKED STEAK SALAD
## WITH SESAME-GINGER DRESSING

**IDEAL GRILL:**

**SMOKE INTENSITY:** moderate

**PREP TIME:** 25 minutes

**COOKING TIME:** 8-10 minutes

**SERVES:** 4

### RUB

2 teaspoons garlic granules

1 teaspoon Chinese five spice

1 teaspoon ground black pepper

1 teaspoon ground coriander

1 teaspoon sea salt

Piece of flank *or* skirt steak,
    750 g–1 kg/1½–2 lb and about
    1.5 cm/¾inch thick

Groundnut oil

2 portobello mushrooms, each
    about 125 g/4 oz, stalks and gills
    removed

### DRESSING

3 tablespoons rice vinegar

2 tablespoons soy sauce

1 tablespoon toasted sesame oil

1 tablespoon peeled, finely chopped
    fresh ginger

1 teaspoon toasted sesame seeds

2 large handfuls hickory wood chips,
    soaked in water for at least 30
    minutes

### SALAD

2 oranges

2 round lettuce, about 500 g/
    1 lb total weight, separated into
    leaves

25 g/1 oz flaked almonds, toasted

4 spring onions (white and light
    green parts only), thinly sliced

*Flank steak has a terrific flavour, but it can be tough because of chewy fibres that run the length of the steak. Cut the steak across those fibres, at right angles to the length of the steak, so you cut those fibres short and effectively make the meat tender.*

1 Combine the rub ingredients in a small bowl. Lightly brush the steak on both sides with groundnut oil and season evenly with the rub. Leave the steak to stand at room temperature for 15–30 minutes before cooking.

2 Prepare a two-zone fire for medium heat (180–230°C/350–450°F) (see pages 20–21).

3 Generously brush each mushroom cap with groundnut oil.

4 Whisk the dressing ingredients in a small bowl, including 3 tablespoons groundnut oil.

5 Brush the cooking grate clean. Drain and add the wood chips to the charcoal and put the lid on the grill. When the wood begins to smoke, cook the steak and mushrooms over **GRILLING/DIRECT MEDIUM HEAT** with the bottom vents closed and the lid vent closed about halfway, turning once or twice, until the steak is medium rare and the mushrooms are tender. Keep the lid firmly closed while cooking. The steak will take 8–10 minutes and the mushrooms will take 6–8 minutes. Remove from the grill and leave the steak to rest for 3–5 minutes.

6 Cut off a small slice from the top and bottom of each orange so the round fruit can stand upright. Use a serrated knife to cut the rind and white pith off the flesh in long arcs, starting at the top and following down along the natural curve of the fruit. Then hold the peeled fruit in your hand and use a paring knife to cut between the flesh and the white membranes separating the individual segments. Allow the segments to fall into a bowl. Discard the membranes, pith and peel.

7 Cut the steak into thin strips and the mushrooms into bite-sized pieces. Divide the lettuce between plates and top with equal amounts of steak, mushrooms, oranges, almonds and spring onions. Drizzle generously with the dressing and serve immediately.

*To toast the almonds, spread them on a baking sheet and bake for about 10 minutes, stirring occasionally, in a preheated 180°C/350°F/Gas mark 4 oven until golden brown and fragrant. Transfer to a plate to cool.*

# OPEN-FACED STEAK SANDWICHES

## WITH GREEN CHILLI SALSA

**IDEAL GRILL:**

**SMOKE INTENSITY:** mild

**PREP TIME:** 30 minutes

**COOKING TIME:** 9–11 minutes

**SERVES:** 8

### RUB

2 teaspoons garlic granules

1 teaspoon sea salt

1 teaspoon ground black pepper

¼ teaspoon ground cayenne pepper

2 flank *or* skirt steaks, each about
    500 g/1 lb and 1.5 cm/¾ inch thick

Extra-virgin olive oil

### SALSA

400 g/13 oz ripe plum tomatoes,
    chopped

4 spring onions (white and light
    green parts only), thinly sliced

125 g/4 oz whole mild green chillies,
    drained, each chilli cut into
    small pieces

2 tablespoons finely chopped fresh
    coriander

1 tablespoon finely chopped garlic

2 teaspoons red wine vinegar

½ teaspoon sea salt

¼ teaspoon hot pepper sauce

8 slices artisan bread, each about
    1 cm/½ inch thick

2 large handfuls oak wood chips,
    soaked in water for at least 30
    minutes

1 Mix the rub ingredients in a small bowl. Lightly brush the steaks on both sides with oil and season evenly with the rub. Leave the steaks to stand at room temperature for 15–30 minutes before cooking.

2 Prepare a two-zone fire for medium heat (180–230°C/350–450°F) (see pages 18–19).

3 Mix the salsa ingredients in a medium, non-reactive bowl and set aside at room temperature. Lightly brush the bread slices on both sides with oil.

4 Brush the cooking grates clean. Drain and add the wood chips to the charcoal and put the lid on the grill. When the wood begins to smoke, cook the steaks over **GRILLING/DIRECT MEDIUM HEAT** with the lid closed as much as possible and turning once or twice, until cooked to your desired doneness, 8–10 minutes for medium rare keeping the lid firmly closed. Remove from the grill and leave to rest for 3–5 minutes. While the steaks rest, toast the bread over **GRILLING/DIRECT MEDIUM HEAT** for about 1 minute, turning once.

5 Cut the steaks across the grain into relatively thin slices and lay the slices on the toasted bread. Lightly top the steak with salsa and serve warm or at room temperature.

*If you want to add even more flavour, rub the bread slices with a clove of garlic immediately after toasting them.*

# DIJON AND GARLIC RIB-EYES
## SMOKED WITH A LITTLE THYME

**IDEAL GRILL:**

**SMOKE INTENSITY:** mild

**PREP TIME:** 15 minutes

**MARINATING TIME:** 2–4 hours

**COOKING TIME:** 6–8 minutes

**SERVES:** 4–6

### PASTE
1 small handful thyme sprigs
3 tablespoons extra-virgin olive oil
1 tablespoon Dijon mustard
1 tablespoon balsamic vinegar
1 tablespoon finely chopped garlic
½ teaspoon celery seed
Sea salt
Ground black pepper

4 boneless rib-eye steaks, each
    375–500 g/12–16 oz and about 2.5
    cm/1 inch thick
2 small handfuls hickory or mesquite
    wood chips, soaked in water for at
    least 30 minutes

*To grill steaks evenly, make sure the charcoal extends at least 10 cm/4 inches beyond the outer edge of each steak, and when you turn the steaks, swap their positions.*

**1** Strip the leaves from the thyme sprigs and reserve the sprigs for tossing on the coals later. Finely chop enough of the leaves to give you 2 tablespoons of chopped thyme. Mix the thyme leaves in a small bowl with the remaining paste ingredients, including 1 teaspoon salt and ¼ teaspoon pepper.

**2** Brush the paste evenly over both sides of the steaks. Cover and refrigerate for 2–4 hours.

**3** Remove the steaks from the refrigerator and season evenly with ½ teaspoon salt and ¼ teaspoon pepper. Leave the steaks to stand at room temperature for 15–30 minutes before cooking.

**4** Prepare a two-zone fire for high heat (230–290°C/450–550°F) (see pages 20–21).

**5** Brush the cooking grate clean. Drain and add the wood chips and thyme sprigs to the charcoal and put the lid on the grill. When smoke appears, grill the steaks over **GRILLING/DIRECT HIGH HEAT** with the lid closed as much as possible and turning once or twice, until cooked to your desired doneness, 6–8 minutes for medium rare, keeping the lid firmly closed. Remove from the grill and leave to rest for 3–5 minutes. Serve warm.

# PECAN-SMOKED VEAL CHOPS
## WITH SAUTÉED LEEK AND MUSHROOMS

IDEAL
GRILL:

**SMOKE INTENSITY:** strong

**PREP TIME:** 20 minutes

**COOKING TIME:** 6–8 minutes

**SERVES:** 4

*The wet tarragon paste is truly delicious, but all that moisture prevents browning, so start searing the chops on at least one side first, and then begin brushing with the paste.*

### PASTE
4 tablespoons finely chopped fresh
    tarragon
2 tablespoons wholegrain mustard
2 tablespoons toasted hazelnut oil *or*
    walnut oil *or* extra-virgin olive oil
2 tablespoons dry white wine *or* dry
    vermouth

4 veal rib chops, each about
    375–500 g/12–16 oz and about
    2.5 cm/1 inch thick
1 tablespoon vegetable oil
Sea salt
Ground black pepper

1 large handful pecan wood chips,
    soaked in water for at least
    30 minutes

50 g/2 oz unsalted butter
1 small leek (white and light green
    parts only), washed well to
    remove any dirt, thinly sliced
500g/1 lb shiitake mushrooms, stalks
    removed, caps thinly sliced
4 tablespoons dry white wine *or* dry
    vermouth
1 teaspoon wholegrain mustard

**1** Mix the paste ingredients in a small bowl.

**2** Lightly brush the veal chops on both sides with the vegetable oil and season evenly with 2 teaspoons salt and ½ teaspoon pepper. Leave the chops to stand at room temperature for 15–30 minutes before cooking.

**3** Prepare a two-zone fire for medium heat (180–230°C/350–450°F) (see pages 20–21).

**4** Brush the cooking grate clean. Drain and add the wood chips to the charcoal and put the lid on the grill. When the wood begins to smoke, place the chops over **GRILLING/DIRECT MEDIUM HEAT**. Brush the tops of the chops with half of the paste, put the lid on the grill, and cook for 3–4 minutes. Turn the chops over and brush them with the remaining paste. Continue to cook for a further 3–4 minutes, until the chops are slightly pink in the centre. Remove from the grill and leave to rest while you prepare the leek and mushrooms.

**5** Melt half the butter in a large frying pan over a medium heat. Add the leek and cook for about 2 minutes until softened. Add the mushrooms and cook for about 3 minutes, stirring occasionally, until they are dry. Pour in the wine and bring to the boil. Remove from the heat. Add the remaining butter and the mustard. Using a wooden spoon, stir until the butter emulsifies into a creamy sauce. Season with salt and pepper. Top the chops with the leek, mushrooms and sauce and serve immediately.

# MOROCCAN SMOKE-ROASTED BEEF SIRLOIN

**IDEAL GRILL:**

**SMOKE INTENSITY:** moderate

**PREP TIME:** 20 minutes

**COOKING TIME:** about 42 minutes

**SPECIAL EQUIPMENT:** spice mill or pestle and mortar, kitchen string, large disposable roasting tray, instant-read meat thermometer

**SERVES:** 6–8

## RUB

1½ teaspoons caraway seeds

1½ teaspoons coriander seeds

1½ teaspoons cumin seeds

1½ teaspoons soft dark brown sugar, preferably muscovado teaspoon sea salt

¼ teaspoon ground cinnamon

¼ teaspoon ground black pepper

⅛ teaspoon ground cloves

1 beef sirloin joint, about 1.5 kg/ 3 lb, trimmed of silver skin and excess fat

2 tablespoons extra-virgin olive oil

2 large handfuls mesquite wood chips, soaked in water for at least 30 minutes

*Sear the beef joint when the coals reach the high end of the medium heat temperature range, 230°C/450°F. By the time the roast is seared over grilling/ direct heat, the temperature of the grill will be in the middle of the range and ready to continue cooking with roasting/indirect heat.*

**1** Coarsely grind the caraway, coriander and cumin seeds in a spice mill or pestle and mortar (or crush the seeds on a chopping board under a heavy saucepan). Pour into a small bowl and mix in the remaining rub ingredients.

**2** Tie the joint with kitchen string every 5 cm/2 inches to make it even and compact. Lightly coat with the oil and season evenly with the rub. Leave the meat to stand at room temperature for 15–30 minutes before cooking.

**3** Prepare a two-zone fire for medium-high heat (200–260°C/400°–500°F) (see pages 20–21). Place a large disposable foil tray beside the bed of charcoal and fill three-quarters full with water.

**4** Brush the cooking grate clean. Sear the meat over **GRILLING/DIRECT MEDIUM-HIGH HEAT** for about 12 minutes, with the lid closed as much as possible, turning a quarter turn once every 3–4 minutes.

**5** Slide the meat over **ROASTING/INDIRECT MEDIUM-HIGH HEAT**, directly over the foil tray. Drain and add the wood chips to the charcoal. Close the lid and cook until an instant-read meat thermometer inserted into the centre of the thickest part of the joint registers 52°C/125°F for medium rare, about 30 minutes. Transfer to a carving board and leave to rest for 10–15 minutes (the internal temperature will rise 5–10 degrees during this time).

**6** Remove the string and cut the roast across into 1-cm/½-inch slices. Serve warm.

# PEPPERY BEEF JERKY

IDEAL
GRILL:

SMOKE INTENSITY: moderate

FREEZING TIME: 1-2 hours

MARINATING TIME: 1 hour

COOKING TIME: 6-7 hours

SPECIAL EQUIPMENT: pestle and
mortar

SERVES: 12

1 beef topside joint, about 1 kg/
  2 lb, silver skin and external fat
  removed

## MARINADE
4 tablespoons soy sauce
2 tablespoons Worcestershire sauce
1 tablespoon runny honey

## RUB
2 teaspoons black peppercorns
2 teaspoons green peppercorns
2 teaspoons pink peppercorns
2 teaspoons white peppercorns
2 teaspoons Sichuan peppercorns

1 large handful hickory wood chunks

*Once the initial smoke wears off, you need no more. The rest of the cooking is simply about drying out the meat.*

**1** Freeze the meat for 1-2 hours until frosty but not hard. Place the joint on a chopping board with the flat end facing right or left, depending on your dominant hand. Starting at the flat end, cut off 5-mm-¼-inch-thick slices.

**2** Whisk the marinade ingredients in a large bowl until thoroughly blended. Add the beef slices and turn to coat. Refrigerate, uncovered, for 1 hour.

**3** Meanwhile, coarsely crush the peppercorns using a pestle and mortar (or crush them on a chopping board under a heavy saucepan). Pour into a small bowl and mix thoroughly.

**4** Remove the beef slices from the bowl and spread them out flat on a large roasting tray. Discard the marinade. Season the slices evenly with half of the rub, pressing the pepper into the meat. Turn the slices over and repeat.

**5** Prepare the smoker for roasting/indirect cooking with extremely low heat (about 80°C/175°F) (see pages 23–25). Use only about half of a chimney starter full of charcoal briquettes.

**6** Brush the cooking grate clean. Add the wood chunks to the charcoal. Smoke the beef slices over **ROASTING/INDIRECT EXTREMELY LOW HEAT** for 6–7 hours, with the lid closed, until they are dry and almost brittle. Add lit briquettes (the heat is too low in the smoker to ignite unlit briquettes) to the charcoal to keep the heat low and even. Transfer the jerky to a serving plate and allow to cool.

**7** Serve within 2 hours of removing from the smoker. Store leftovers in an airtight container in the refrigerator for up to 2 weeks, or wrap airtight and freeze for up to 4 months.

# SPICED AND SMOKED BRAISED BEEF

**IDEAL
GRILL:**

**SMOKE INTENSITY:** moderate

**PREP TIME:** 15 minutes, plus
about 25 minutes for the sauce

**BRAISING TIME:** about 2 hours

**COOLING TIME:** about 4 hours

**COOKING TIME:** about 1 hour

**SPECIAL EQUIPMENT:** large
disposable roasting tray, instant-
read meat thermometer

**SERVES:** 6

## BRAISING LIQUID
3.5 litres/6 pints water
2 tablespoons coriander seeds
2 tablespoons black peppercorns
1 tablespoon cardamom pods
1 tablespoon sea salt
2 whole star anise
1 cinnamon stick

1 beef brisket joint, about 1.8 kg/
   3¾ lb, rolled and tied

## SAUCE
1 tablespoon vegetable oil
1 small onion, finely chopped
2 tablespoons peeled, finely chopped
   fresh ginger
2 teaspoons finely chopped garlic
240 ml/8 fl oz ketchup
240 ml/8 fl oz ketchup-style chilli
   sauce *or* bottled barbecue sauce
120 ml/4 fl oz sherry vinegar *or* cider
   vinegar
125 g/4 oz soft light brown sugar
75 ml/3 fl oz water
5 tablespoons wholegrain mustard
⅛ teaspoon hot pepper sauce

2 large handfuls mesquite wood
   chips, soaked in water for at least
   30 minutes

*The meat can be covered and refrigerated for up to 1 day after braising and
cooling. Allow to stand at room temperature for 1 hour before cooking.*

**1** Bring the braising liquid ingredients to the boil in a large stockpot over a high
heat, Add the beef joint and add more water to cover, if needed. Return to the
boil and reduce the heat to medium-low. Cover and simmer the meat for about
2 hours until the internal temperature reaches 85°C/185°F.

**2** Transfer the joint to a plate and discard the braising liquid. Leave to stand at
room temperature for about 2 hours until cooled. Wrap the meat in clingfilm and
refrigerate for at least 2 hours until chilled. Meanwhile, make the sauce.

**3** Warm the oil in a medium saucepan over a medium heat. Add the onion, ginger
and garlic and cook for about 3 minutes, stirring often, until the onion is tender.
Add the remaining sauce ingredients and bring to a simmer. Reduce the heat
to medium-low and cook for about 20 minutes, stirring often, until thickened.
Remove from the heat and leave the sauce to cool.

**4** Prepare a two-zone fire for low heat (130–180°C/250–350°F) (see pages 20–21).
Place a large disposable foil tray beside the bed of charcoal and fill three-
quarters full with water. Maintain the temperature between 170 and 180°C/325°
and 350°F.

**5** Brush the cooking grate clean. Drain and add one handful of the wood chips to
the charcoal and put the lid on the grill. When the wood begins to smoke, cook
the meat over **ROASTING/INDIRECT LOW HEAT** for 30 minutes, with the lid closed.
Drain and add the remaining wood chips to the charcoal and continue cooking
over **ROASTING/INDIRECT LOW HEAT** for about 30 minutes more, with the lid
closed, until the meat is heated through and the internal temperature reaches
60°C/140°F. During the last 10 minutes, brush the meat with some of the sauce.
Transfer to a chopping board, tent with foil and leave to rest for about 10 minutes
(the internal temperature will rise 5–10 degrees during this time).

**6** Cut the meat against the grain into thin slices. Serve with the remaining sauce
and some white bread, if liked. Serving suggestion: Classic Coleslaw (for the
recipe, see page 197).

# SMOKY BRAISED BEEF CHILLI

**IDEAL GRILL:**

**SMOKE INTENSITY:** moderate

**PREP TIME:** 30 minutes

**COOKING TIME:** about 2¼ hours

**SPECIAL EQUIPMENT:** large saucepan suitable for the grill

**SERVES:** 6

*If you like beans in your chilli, by all means add them. Two 475-g/15-oz cans of pinto or pink beans, rinsed, added to the pan during the last 15 minutes of cooking, will make a very thick chilli.*

2 rolled beef brisket joints, each about 1 kg/2 lb
3 tablespoons extra-virgin olive oil
Sea salt
Ground black pepper

4 mesquite wood chunks

2 onions, roughly chopped
2 peppers, 1 green and 1 red, cut into 1-cm/½-inch pieces
4 garlic cloves, finely chopped
1 serrano chilli, deseeded and finely chopped
4 tablespoons prepared chilli seasoning
2 teaspoons dried oregano
2 teaspoons ground cumin
2 x 425-g/14-oz can plum tomatoes in juice, roughly chopped
350 ml/12 fl oz beer (not stout)

1 Prepare a two-zone fire for high heat (230–290°C/450–550°F) (see pages 20–21).

2 Cut each joint in half. Brush with 1 tablespoon of the oil and season evenly with 1½ teaspoons salt and ¾ teaspoon pepper. Leave the meat to stand at room temperature for 15–30 minutes before cooking.

3 Brush the cooking grate clean. Add two wood chunks to the charcoal and put the lid on the grill. When the wood begins to smoke, cook the meat over **GRILLING/ DIRECT HIGH HEAT** for about 6 minutes, with the lid closed as much as possible and turning once, until browned on both sides. Move the roasts over **ROASTING/ INDIRECT HIGH HEAT** and continue cooking while you cook the vegetables.

4 In a large saucepan suitable for the grill combine the remaining 2 tablespoons oil with the onions, peppers, garlic and chilli. Cook over **GRILLING/DIRECT HIGH HEAT** for 8–10 minutes, with the lid closed as much as possible and stirring occasionally, until the onions are tender. Add the chilli seasoning, oregano and cumin and stir well. Stir in the tomatoes with their juice and the beer. Transfer the meat to the pan and bring the mixture to a simmer. Cover the pan with its lid or cover tightly with aluminium foil. By this time, the coals should have burned down to about 180°C/350°F. Move the pan over **ROASTING/INDIRECT MEDIUM HEAT**, close the lid, and cook for about 2 hours until the meat is so tender it falls apart. After 1 hour, add more lit briquettes to maintain the heat and add the two remaining wood chunks to the charcoal. Remove the pan from the grill, remove the lid and leave to rest for about 5 minutes. Skim off any fat from the surface. Using two forks, pull the meat into bite-sized pieces. Season with salt and pepper. Serve hot.

# KOREAN TOP RUMP
## WITH QUICK PICKLED VEGETABLES

**IDEAL GRILL:**

**SMOKE INTENSITY:** moderate

**PREP TIME:** 30 minutes

**MARINATING TIME:** 8–24 hours

**COOKING TIME:** 23–30 minutes

**SERVES:** 4

### MARINADE

1 Asian pear *or* ordinary pear, about
    250 g/8 oz, coarsely grated
125 g/4 oz thinly sliced spring onions
    (white and light green parts only)
4 tablespoons dry sherry
4 tablespoons soy sauce
2 tablespoons soft light brown sugar
1½ tablespoons roughly chopped
    garlic
1 tablespoon sesame seeds
1 tablespoon toasted sesame oil
½ teaspoon crushed red chilli flakes

1 beef rump roast, 750 g–1 kg/
    1½–2 lb, excess fat and silver skin
    removed

### VEGETABLES

75 ml/3 fl oz rice vinegar
1 tablespoon granulated sugar
2 teaspoons sea salt
2 carrots, about 175 g/6 oz total
    weight, cut into very thin strips
1 piece daikon (white radish), about
    175 g/6 oz, cut into very thin strips

1 large handful oak or apple wood
    chips, soaked in water for at least
    30 minutes

1 Whisk the marinade ingredients in a medium bowl until the sugar is dissolved. Place the meat in a large, resealable plastic bag and pour in the marinade. Press the air out of the bag and seal tightly. Turn the bag to distribute the marinade and refrigerate for 8–24 hours, turning once or twice. Leave the meat to stand at room temperature for about 30 minutes before cooking.

2 Whisk the vinegar, sugar and salt in a medium bowl. Add the carrots and daikon and toss to coat. Cover and leave to stand at room temperature for at least 30 minutes or up to 2 hours. Drain the vegetables just before serving.

3 Prepare a two-zone fire for medium heat (180–230°C/350–450°F) (see pages 20–21).

4 Remove the meat from the bag and discard the marinade. Brush the cooking grate clean. Drain and add the wood chips to the charcoal and put the lid on the grill. When the wood begins to smoke, cook the roast over **GRILLING/DIRECT MEDIUM HEAT** for 8–10 minutes, with the lid closed as much as possible and turning once or twice, until well marked on both sides. Then move the meat over **ROASTING/INDIRECT MEDIUM HEAT**, close the lid and continue cooking until it reaches your desired doneness, 15–20 minutes for medium rare. Remove from the grill and leave to rest for 5–10 minutes.

5 Cut the meat across the grain into thin slices. Serve warm with the pickled vegetables on the side.

# SLOW-SMOKED MESQUITE BRISKET

**IDEAL GRILL:**

**SMOKE INTENSITY:** strong

**PREP TIME:** 45 minutes

**MARINATING TIME:** 12–24 hours

**COOKING TIME:** 7–9 hours

**RESTING TIME:** 1–2 hours

**SPECIAL EQUIPMENT:** food syringe; extra-large disposable foil roasting tray; instant-read meat thermometer

**SERVINGS:** 12–15

1 whole, untrimmed beef brisket,
    5–6 kg/10 –12 lb
240 ml/8 fl oz beef stock
5 tablespoons prepared mustard

## RUB
2 tablespoons chilli powder
1 tablespoon soft light brown sugar
1 tablespoon sea salt
1 tablespoon onion powder
1 tablespoon paprika
1 tablespoon ground cumin
2 teaspoons ground black pepper
2 teaspoons ground allspice

8 fist-sized mesquite wood chunks

*Plan on a full day of cooking time. Yes, it takes time to make that cut of meat tender and delicious. For this big piece of meat, you will need a big smoker. A 55-cm/22½-inch-diameter Smokey Mountain Cooker™ smoker works very well for this, but the 45-cm/18-inch version is too small.*

*Plan ahead. First you will need to find and purchase a very large piece of meat, at least 5–6 kg/10–12 lb, which you might need to order from a butcher. The quality of the meat is the most important part of the recipe. Do not try to barbecue a low-quality brisket; it will be tough and dry. Buy top-quality beef from a reputable supplier. You need a full, untrimmed brisket that includes a flat, relatively lean section and a thicker, fattier section. When you lift the brisket up from the fattier end, the lean section should flop over easily, indicating there is not too much connective tissue making the meat tight and tough.*

1 The night before you smoke the brisket, trim it. Using a very sharp knife on the fat side, trim the fat so that it is about 8 mm/⅓ inch thick, but no less. On the meatier side, remove the web-like membrane that covers the meat, so that you can clearly see (and eventually season) the coarsely grained meat underneath. Then, using a food syringe, inject the meat with the beef stock: With the fat side facing down in an extra-large foil roasting tray, imagine the brisket in 2.5-cm/1-inch squares and inject each square with some of the stock, inserting the needle parallel to the grain of the meat and slowly pulling the needle out as you inject the stock (see photo on facing page). Some stock will seep out, but try to keep as much as possible inside the meat. Then smear the mustard over both sides of the brisket.

2 Mix the rub ingredients in a small bowl. Massage the rub all over the brisket creating a paste with the mustard and stock. Turn the brisket so that the fat side is facing up. Cover the tray and refrigerate for at least 12 hours or up to 24 hours. Remove the brisket from the refrigerator and leave to stand in the tray at room temperature for 1 hour before smoking.

3 Prepare the smoker for roasting/indirect cooking with very low heat (95–130°C/200–250°F) (see pages 23–25).

4 Add two wood chunks to the charcoal. Smoke the brisket over the pan on the cooking grate over **ROASTING/INDIRECT VERY LOW HEAT** for 4 hours, with the lid closed, adjusting the vents so the temperature inside the smoker stays as close to 110°C/225°F as possible. At the start of the second, third and fourth hours, add two more wood chunks to the charcoal and baste the brisket with any liquid that accumulates in the pan.

5 After 4 hours, use an instant-read meat thermometer to check the internal temperature of the meat. If it has not reached 70°C/160°F, continue cooking until it does. If it has reached 70°C/160°F, remove the brisket in the tray from the smoker. Put the lid back on the smoker to prevent heat loss. Add more lit briquettes and refill the water pan to maintain the 110°C/225°F temperature.

6 Lay out three sheets of heavy-duty aluminium foil on a large work surface, each about 90 cm/3 feet long, overlapping the sheets slightly along their longer sides. Place the brisket in the centre of the foil, fat side up. Pour 8 tablespoons of the liquid in the tray over the meat, and fold up the edges to wrap the brisket tightly to trap the steam. At this point you can discard the remaining liquid that has accumulated in the tray, though some people like to save it for adding to their barbecue sauce.

**7** Return the brisket to the tray, fat side facing up, and return the tray to the smoker. Cook over **ROASTING/INDIRECT VERY LOW HEAT** for at least 3 hours and as long as 5 hours, with the lid closed, until the meat is so tender that when you insert the probe of an instant-read meat thermometer and push it back and forth, it easily tears the meat. The internal temperature should be 88–90°C/190°–195°F, though tenderness is a more important indicator of doneness than the temperature. The amount of time required will depend on the particular breed and other characteristics of the meat. Remove from the smoker and leave the brisket to rest at room temperature for 1–2 hours.

**8** Unwrap the brisket and cut across the grain into thin slices. Serve warm with your favourite barbecue sauce and side dishes, such as Cider and Bacon Beans (see page 191). If you have any leftover brisket, use it to make Barbecued Brisket Tamales (see page 89).

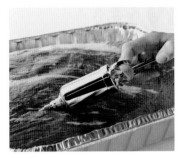

*With the needle running parallel to the grain of the meat, inject the stock as evenly as you can. As you press the plunger, slowly draw the needle to the surface of the meat, and then insert the needle in a nearby spot.*

# BARBECUED BRISKET TAMALES

**PREP TIME:** 1 hour

**STEAMING TIME:** 1½ hours

**SPECIAL EQUIPMENT:** electric food mixer, deep saucepan, large steamer insert

**SERVES:** 12

## SAUCE
2 tablespoons extra-virgin olive oil
1 red onion, finely chopped
1 tablespoon finely chopped garlic
250 g/8 oz canned chopped tomatoes
240 ml/8 fl oz Mexican lager
2 dried pasilla chillies, stemmed, deseeded and cut into strips
1 tablespoon cider vinegar
1 teaspoon dried oregano
1 teaspoon ground cumin
½ teaspoon sea salt

75 g/3 oz packet dried corn husks for tamales (48 husks)

750 g/1½ lb smoked brisket (see page 86)

625 g/1¼ lb instant masa harina
2 teaspoons baking powder
2 teaspoons sea salt
1 litre/1¾ pints warm water
325 ml/11 fl oz melted lard
Soured cream
Chopped fresh coriander

*To be on the safe side, soak extra corn husks. Some will tear, some will not be big enough, and some can be used to patch holes in the husks you're using. There are about 48 husks in a 75-g/3-oz bag, so just soak them all.*

1 Warm the oil in a medium, heavy saucepan over a medium heat. Add the onion and cook for about 3 minutes, stirring occasionally, until softened. Add the garlic and cook for about 2 minutes until golden. Stir in the remaining sauce ingredients and bring to the boil. Reduce the heat to medium-low and simmer, uncovered for about 20 minutes, stirring often, until slightly thickened. Remove from the heat and cover. Leave to stand for 15 minutes to soften the chillies. Purée in a blender or with a stick blender.

2 Set the corn husks in a deep saucepan. Cover them with boiling water. Set a small plate on top of the husks to keep them submerged in the water. Steep for about 30 minutes until softened.

3 Pulse the pieces of brisket in a food processor fitted with a metal chopping blade until coarsely minced. Scrape into a large bowl, add 180 ml/6 fl oz of the sauce (reserve the remaining sauce for serving), and stir until well combined.

4 Combine the masa harina, baking powder and salt in the bowl of an electric mixer. Add the water and lard, then stir and beat with the paddle attachment on low speed to make a firm, spongy dough.

5 Drain the husks well. Tear a couple of the husks lengthways to make 40 thin strips for tying the folded tamales. For each tamale, place a husk on the work surface, curved side facing up with the pointed end facing away from you. Spread about 3 generous tablespoons of the masa dough into the centre of the husk; smear the dough into a rough rectangle about 10 cm/4 inches wide by 7 cm/3 inches long, leaving a border at the longer edge of the husk. Spoon 1–2 tablespoons of the brisket mixture in a line down the centre of the dough. Bring the two long sides of the husk together to enclose the filling with the masa, and pinch the seam closed. Wrap the tamale in the husk. Fold the pointed end of the husk up. Using a husk strip, tie and secure the folded husk in place, leaving the top of the tamale open (see photo at bottom left).

6 Set up a large steamer insert or a steaming basket in a deep saucepan. Add enough water to almost reach, but not touch, the bottom of the steamer. Stand the tamales, open ends up, on the steamer. (The tamales should support each other to stand, but not be packed together.) Cover the pan tightly and bring the water to the boil over a high heat. Reduce the heat to medium-low to maintain a steady head of steam in the pan. Steam for about 1½ hours until the tamale dough has lost its raw look and taste and is firm enough to easily pull away from the husk. Add more hot water to the pan as needed.

7 Reheat the reserved sauce and transfer to a serving bowl. Serve the tamales warm with the sauce, soured cream and coriander.

*Any smoked meat will work in this recipe. Next time try chicken or pork.*

# PECAN-SMOKED LAMB SHOULDER
## WITH VEGETABLE COUSCOUS

IDEAL GRILL:

SMOKE INTENSITY: moderate

PREP TIME: 30 minutes

REFRIGERATION TIME: 12–24 hours

COOKING TIME: about 2¼ hours

SPECIAL EQUIPMENT: kitchen string, instant-read meat thermometer

SERVES: 6

### PASTE
4 tablespoons extra-virgin olive oil
4 tablespoons fresh thyme
4 garlic cloves, finely chopped
1½ teaspoons crushed red chilli flakes
1 teaspoon sea salt
½ teaspoon ground black pepper

1 boneless lamb shoulder, about 1.75 kg/3½ lb, trimmed of excess fat

2 large handfuls pecan wood chips, soaked in water for at least 30 minutes

25 g/1 oz tablespoons unsalted butter
4 spring onions (white and light green parts only), thinly sliced
1 red pepper, finely chopped
1 small courgette, ends trimmed, finely chopped
2 teaspoons finely chopped oregano *or* 1 teaspoon dried oregano
1 teaspoon paprika
¾ teaspoon sea salt
½ teaspoon ground black pepper
750 ml/1¼ pints chicken stock
275 g/9 oz quick-cooking couscous

1 Combine the paste ingredients in a food processor and process until smooth.

2 Place the lamb, smooth side down, on a work surface. Spread the paste in a thick layer over the rough side (the side that faced the bone) of the lamb. Starting at a long end, roll the lamb into a thick cylinder. Tie with kitchen string to hold its shape. Place in a large, resealable plastic bag and refrigerate for 12–24 hours.

3 Prepare the grill for roasting/indirect cooking over medium heat (180–230°C/350–450°F) (see pages 26–27).

4 Remove the lamb from the bag. Brush the cooking grates clean. Drain and add one handful of the wood chips to the smoker box of a gas grill, following manufacturer's instructions, and close the lid. When the wood begins to smoke, cook the lamb over **ROASTING/INDIRECT MEDIUM HEAT** for 1 hour, with the lid closed. After the first hour, drain and add the remaining wood chips to the smoker box. Close the lid and continue to cook for about 1¼ hours more until the internal temperature reaches 68°C/155°F. Remove from the grill and wrap tightly in aluminium foil. Leave the lamb to rest for 10–15 minutes (the internal temperature will rise 5–10 degrees during this time). While the lamb is resting, make the couscous.

5 Melt the butter in a large saucepan over a medium heat. Add the spring onions, pepper and courgette and cook for about 4 minutes, stirring often, until slightly softened. Stir in the oregano, paprika, salt and pepper. Add the stock and bring to the boil over a high heat. Stir in the couscous. Remove from the heat and cover tightly. Leave to stand for about 5 minutes until the liquid has been absorbed. Fluff the couscous with a fork.

6 Unwrap the lamb, remove the string, and cut across the grain into slices. Spoon the couscous on to dinner plates, and top with the lamb and the carving juices.

*Use the paste in this recipe to season a boneless leg of lamb, about 2.5 kg/4½ lb, and cook according to the directions for the recipe on page 93.*

# OAK-ROASTED LEG OF LAMB
## WITH HAZELNUT GREMOLATA

**IDEAL GRILL:**

**SMOKE INTENSITY:** moderate

**PREP TIME:** 30 minutes

**COOKING TIME:** about 1 hour

**SPECIAL EQUIPMENT:** kitchen string, large disposable foil tray, instant-read meat thermometer

**SERVES:** 8

### GREMOLATA

100g/3½ oz hazelnuts

2 garlic cloves

50 g/ 2 oz flat-leaf parsley, leaves and tender stems

Finely grated zest of 2 lemons

Sea salt

Ground black pepper

1 boneless leg of lamb, about 2.25 kg/4½ lb, trimmed of any excess fat and sinew, butterflied

Extra-virgin olive oil

2 large handfuls oak wood chips, soaked in water for at least 30 minutes

*Grapevines would be an excellent alternative for the oak wood chips.*

1 Preheat the oven to 180°C/350°F/Gas mark 4. Spread the hazelnuts on a baking sheet. Bake for about 10 minutes, stirring occasionally, until the skins are cracked. Transfer to a clean tea towel and let cool for 10 minutes. Wrap and rub the cooled nuts in the towel to remove the skins (some skin will remain); roughly chop them.

2 Chop the garlic in a food processor. Add the hazelnuts, parsley, lemon zest, ½ teaspoon salt and ½ teaspoon pepper. Pulse into a coarse paste.

3 Place the lamb, cut side up, on a work surface. Using a sharp knife, make angled, deep cuts in the thickest parts of the meat, taking care not to cut all the way through, and spread the flaps open like a book. When you are finished, the lamb should be about 1.5 cm/¾ inch thick. Spread the gremolata evenly over the cut surface of the lamb. Starting at a short end, roll up the lamb. Tie the roll crossways in several places with kitchen string. Brush the outside of the lamb with oil and season evenly with 1 teaspoon salt and ½ teaspoon pepper. Set aside at room temperature while you prepare the grill.

4 Prepare a two-zone fire for medium heat (180–230°C/350–450°F) (see pages 20–22). Place a large disposable foil tray beside the bed of charcoal and fill three-quarters full with water.

5 Brush the cooking grate clean. Sear the lamb over **GRILLING/DIRECT MEDIUM HEAT** for about 12 minutes, with the lid closed as much as possible, turning occasionally, until nicely browned on all sides.

6 Drain half of the wood chips and add them to the charcoal. Set the lamb over the foil tray and put the lid on the grill. Grill over **ROASTING/INDIRECT MEDIUM HEAT** for 30 minutes. Drain and add the remaining wood chips to the charcoal. If necessary, add more lit charcoal to maintain the temperature. Cover and continue cooking for about 20 minutes until an instant-read meat thermometer inserted in the thickest part of the lamb reaches 55°C/130°F for medium rare.

7 Transfer the lamb to a carving board and leave to rest for 10–15 minutes (the internal temperature will rise 5–10 degrees during this time). Cut the lamb crossways into 1 cm/½-inch-thick slices. Remove the string and serve warm.

*Do not untie the lamb before carving. The kitchen string will keep the roast secure, the better to cut even slices.*

# ANCHO-MARINATED LEG OF LAMB
## WITH TOMATO-CUCUMBER SALSA

**IDEAL GRILL:**

**SMOKE INTENSITY:** moderate

**PREP TIME:** 30 minutes

**MARINATING TIME:** 12–24 hours

**DRAINING TIME:** 1 hour

**COOKING TIME:** about 1½ hours

**SPECIAL EQUIPMENT:** large disposable foil tray, instant-read meat thermometer

**SERVES:** 6

### MARINADE

2 dried ancho chillies, stems and
    seeds removed
75 ml/3 fl oz red wine vinegar
75 ml/3 fl oz fresh lemon juice
75 ml/3 fl oz extra-virgin olive oil
1 tablespoon ground cumin
1 tablespoon dried oregano
1 tablespoon sea salt
1 tablespoon finely chopped garlic

1 part-boned leg of lamb, about
    2.5 kg/5 lb

### SALSA

4 large plum tomatoes, about
    500 g/1 lb total weight, cut into
    5-mm/¼-inch pieces
1 cucumber, about 300 g/10 oz, cut
    into ¼-inch dice
Sea salt
75 g/3 oz feta cheese, crumbled
2 tablespoons red wine vinegar
2 tablespoons chopped fresh
    coriander
½ teaspoon finely chopped garlic
Ground black pepper

4 large handfuls mesquite wood
    chips, soaked in water for at least
    30 minutes

1 Toast the chillies in a medium, heavy frying pan over a medium-high heat for 2–3 minutes, turning occasionally, until they are lightly charred, pliable and dark brick red in spots. Transfer to a plate and leave to cool. Put the chillies in a food processor or blender and pulse until you have a coarse powder. Pour the powder into a medium bowl and whisk with the remaining marinade ingredients.

2 Place the lamb in a large, resealable plastic bag and pour in the marinade. Press the air out of the bag and seal tightly. Turn the bag to distribute the marinade, place in a large bowl, and refrigerate for 12–24 hours, turning the bag occasionally.

3 Toss the tomatoes and cucumber with 1 teaspoon salt in a colander and leave to drain for 1 hour. Combine the tomatoes and cucumber with the remaining salsa ingredients In a medium bowl and season with salt and pepper. Cover and refrigerate until ready to serve.

4 Remove the lamb from the bag and discard the marinade. Leave the lamb to stand at room temperature for 30 minutes before cooking.

5 Prepare a two-zone fire for medium heat (180–230°C/350–450°F) (see pages 20–22). Place a large disposable foil tray beside the bed of charcoal and fill three-quarters full with water.

6 Brush the cooking grate clean. Drain and add two handfuls of the wood chips to the charcoal and put the lid on the grill. When the wood begins to smoke, cook the lamb over **ROASTING/INDIRECT MEDIUM HEAT** for 45 minutes, with the lid closed. Turn the lamb over; drain and add the remaining wood chips to the charcoal. Continue cooking, with the lid closed, until the lamb reaches an internal temperature of 55°C/130°F, 40 to 50 minutes for medium rare. Remove from the grill and leave to rest for 10–15 minutes (the internal temperature will rise 5–10 degrees during this time).

7 Cut the lamb across the grain into 1cm/½-inch slices. Serve warm with the salsa.

*A part-boned leg of lamb has had the hip bone and the shank removed, which makes for easier cutting.*

# SMOKED RACKS OF LAMB
## WITH PEPPER AND AUBERGINE AJVAR

IDEAL GRILL:

**SMOKE INTENSITY:** moderate

**PREP TIME:** 20 minutes

**COOKING TIME:** about 40 minutes

**SERVES:** 4

## AJVAR
2 large rounded aubergines, about 300 g/10 oz
1 red pepper, about 250 g/8 oz
1 garlic clove
2 tablespoons fresh lemon juice
1 tablespoon chopped flat-leaf parsley
75 ml/3 fl oz extra-virgin olive oil
Sea salt
Ground black pepper

## RUB
1 teaspoon cumin seeds
1 teaspoon coriander seeds, lightly crushed
1 teaspoon dried oregano
1 teaspoon sea salt
½ teaspoon paprika
½ teaspoon garlic granules
½ teaspoon ground black pepper
½ teaspoon crushed red chilli flakes

2 racks of lamb, each 500–750 g/ 1–1½ lb, frenched and trimmed of excess fat
1 tablespoon extra-virgin olive oil

2 large handfuls oak wood chips, soaked in water for at least 30 minutes

*To 'french' means to remove the fat from the bones extending from a lamb (or pork) rack or chop, then clean them thoroughly for a nice presentation. Many supermarkets sell racks of lamb with the bones already frenched.*

1 Pierce the aubergines several times with a fork. Cut off the top and bottom of the pepper. Then make one cut down the side and open it up into a large strip. Cut away the ribs and seeds.

2 Prepare a two-zone fire for medium heat (180–230°C/350–450°F) (see pages 20–22).

3 Brush the cooking grate clean. Cook the aubergines over **GRILLING/DIRECT MEDIUM HEAT** for about 20 minutes, with the lid closed as much as possible, turning occasionally, until soft and beginning to collapse. At the same time, cook the pepper, shiny skin side down, over **GRILLING/DIRECT MEDIUM HEAT** for 8–10 minutes (do not turn) until the skin is blackened and blistered. Remove from the grill as they are done. Put the pepper in a small bowl and cover with clingfilm to trap the steam. Leave to stand for about 10 minutes. Remove from the bowl and peel away and discard the charred skin. Cut the aubergines in half lengthways and scoop out the pulp. Discard the skin and any large seed pockets.

4 Whirl the garlic in a food processor until it is finely chopped. Add the aubergine pulp, pepper, lemon juice and parsley and pulse to create a thick sauce. With the machine running, slowly add the oil and process until the *ajvar* is smooth and emulsified. Season with salt and pepper.

5 Combine the rub ingredients in a small bowl. Lightly brush the lamb with the oil and season evenly with the rub. Leave the lamb to stand at room temperature for 15–30 minutes before cooking.

6 Replenish the charcoal if needed to maintain a steady temperature, adding 6–10 lit briquettes after 45 minutes.

7 Drain and add the wood chips to the charcoal and put the lid on the grill. When the wood begins to smoke, cook the lamb, bone side down first, over **GRILLING/ DIRECT MEDIUM HEAT** for 5 minutes, with the lid closed as much as possible and turning once (watch for flare-ups). Move the lamb over **ROASTING/INDIRECT MEDIUM HEAT** and continue cooking to your desired doneness, about 15 minutes more for medium rare, turning once or twice. Remove from the grill and leave to rest for 3–5 minutes. Cut the lamb racks between the bones into individual chops. Serve warm with the *ajvar*.

# BEER-BRAISED AND MESQUITE-SMOKED SHORT RIBS

**IDEAL GRILL:**

**SMOKE INTENSITY:** moderate

**PREP TIME:** 45 minutes

**BRAISING TIME:** about 1½ hours

**CHILLING TIME:** about 2 hours

**REDUCING TIME:** 1–1½ hours

**COOKING TIME:** about 30 minutes

**SPECIAL EQUIPMENT:** large stockpot

**SERVES:** 4

## BRAISING LIQUID

1 tablespoon extra-virgin olive oil
1 large onion, about 300 g/10 oz, roughly chopped
6 garlic cloves, roughly chopped
1 jalapeño chilli pepper, about 25 g/1 oz, roughly chopped (with seeds)
2 teaspoons dried oregano
2 teaspoons cumin seeds
1 teaspoon sea salt
½ teaspoon ground black pepper
3 bottles (each 350 ml/12 fl oz) lager
1 bay leaf

2–5 kg/5 lb meaty beef short ribs

## SAUCE

240 ml/8 fl oz tomato ketchup
2 tablespoons black treacle
1 tablespoon balsamic vinegar
2 teaspoons Worcestershire sauce
Hot pepper sauce (optional)

2 tablespoons extra-virgin olive oil
1 teaspoon sea salt
½ teaspoon ground black pepper

2 large handfuls mesquite wood chips, soaked in water for at least 30 minutes

*Look for individually cut short ribs for this recipe.*

1 Heat the oil in a large stockpot over medium heat. Add the onion, garlic and chilli and cook for about 5 minutes, stirring occasionally, until the onion is tender. Add the oregano, cumin seeds, salt and pepper and cook for about 30 seconds, stirring constantly, until fragrant. Pour in the lager and add the bay leaf. Place the ribs in the braising liquid, meaty side down, and add just enough water to cover them. Bring to the boil over a high heat and then reduce the heat to low. Cover and simmer for about 1½ hours until the ribs are barely tender when pierced with the tip of a knife. Transfer the ribs to a roasting tray to cool. Remove and discard any bones that may have fallen off the ribs in the liquid; reserve the liquid. Cover and refrigerate the cooled ribs for about 2 hours until chilled.

2 Strain the braising liquid through a fine sieve into a large bowl and leave to stand for 10 minutes. Skim the fat from the surface of the liquid. Rinse the pan, pour the liquid back into the pan, and bring to the boil over a high heat. Lower the heat and simmer the liquid for 1–1½ hours until reduced to 175 ml/6 fl oz. Transfer to a medium saucepan. Stir in the ketchup, treacle, balsamic vinegar and Worcestershire sauce. Bring to a simmer over a medium heat, then reduce the heat to low, and simmer for about 5 minutes until the sauce is slightly reduced, stirring often. Remove from the heat and season with hot pepper sauce, if liked. Set aside at room temperature.

3 Prepare a two-zone fire for medium heat (180–230°C/350–450°F) (see pages 20–22).

4 Brush the ribs with the oil and season evenly with the salt and pepper. Brush the cooking grate clean. Drain and add one handful of the wood chips to the charcoal and put the lid on the grill. When the wood begins to smoke, cook the ribs over **ROASTING/INDIRECT MEDIUM HEAT** for about 25 minutes, with the lid closed, until the meat begins to crisp around the edges and the ribs are heated through.

5 Brush the ribs generously with the sauce. Drain and add the remaining wood chips to the charcoal. Move the ribs over **GRILLED/DIRECT MEDIUM HEAT**, close the lid, and continue to cook for about 5 minutes, turning occasionally, until the meat is glazed. Remove from the grill and serve warm with the remaining sauce.

*Be sure the ribs are chilled before cooking them so they have a longer reheating period and can soak up more smoke flavour.*

# BIG BEEF BACK RIBS
## WITH PLUM-RUM BARBECUE SAUCE

**IDEAL GRILL:**

**SMOKE INTENSITY:** strong

**PREP TIME:** 40 minutes

**COOKING TIME:** about 4 hours

**SERVES:** 6

## RUB

2 tablespoons paprika

2 tablespoons soft dark brown sugar, preferably muscovado

2 teaspoons ground cinnamon

2 teaspoons dried thyme

2 teaspoons sea salt

2 teaspoons ground black pepper

1 teaspoon grated nutmeg

½ teaspoon ground allspice

½ teaspoon ground mace

2 racks beef back ribs, each about 2 kg/4 lb

4 tablespoons Worcestershire sauce

8 large hickory wood chunks

## SAUCE

4 large, ripe black plums, about 625 g/1¼ lb total weight, chopped

325 g/11 oz canned chopped tomatoes

2 small shallots, finely chopped

4 tablespoons granulated sugar

4 tablespoons dark rum

4 tablespoons maple syrup

4 tablespoons cider vinegar

2 tablespoons Dijon mustard

2 tablespoons Worcestershire sauce

2 tablespoons peeled, finely chopped fresh ginger

½ teaspoon ground black pepper

¼ teaspoon ground cloves

*Beef back ribs are cut from a rib roast. Don't confuse them with short ribs, which are bigger with much tougher meat.*

**1** Mix the rub ingredients in a small bowl.

**2** Use a round-ended dinner knife to help peel the translucent, papery membrane off the back of the racks. Cut each rack in half to make four slabs. Rub the Worcestershire sauce on to the slabs and then pat and smear the rub all over them. Set aside at room temperature while you prepare the smoker.

**3** Prepare the smoker for roasting/indirect cooking with very low heat (95–130°C/ 200-250°F) (see pages 23-25). When the temperature reaches 110°C/225°F, add two hickory wood chunks to the charcoal.

**4** Brush the cooking grate clean. Smoke the slabs, bone side down, over **ROASTING/INDIRECT VERY LOW HEAT** for about 3½ hours, with the lid closed, until they are just tender. Add more lit briquettes as necessary to maintain a steady, even heat between 95 and 130°C/200 and 250°F, and add two more wood chunks to the charcoal every 45 minutes. Meanwhile, make the sauce.

**5** Whisk the sauce ingredients in a large, heavy saucepan. Bring to the boil over a medium-high heat, stirring occasionally. Reduce the heat to medium-low and simmer, uncovered, for about 20 minutes, stirring often, until the plums are very soft and the sauce has lightly thickened. Remove from the heat and purée in a blender, food processor or with a stick blender until smooth.

**6** After the slabs have been in the smoker for 3½ hours (they will look quite dark), baste their tops with some of the sauce and continue smoking over **ROASTING/ INDIRECT VERY LOW HEAT** for about 15 minutes, with the lid closed. Turn the slabs over, baste with more sauce, and cook for about 15 minutes more until the slabs are glazed and tender. Remove from the smoker and leave to rest for about 10 minutes. Cut between the bones and serve the ribs warm with the remaining sauce.

*To tell if the beef ribs are tender, insert a meat fork into the meat between the bones. It should go in very easily.*

# PEPPER-CRUSTED FORE RIB
## WITH THREE-HERB HAZELNUT PESTO

**IDEAL GRILL:**

**SMOKE INTENSITY:** moderate

**PREP TIME:** 30 minutes

**COOKING TIME:** about 2¼ hours

**SPECIAL EQUIPMENT:** instant-read meat thermometer

**SERVES:** 6–8

2 tablespoons coarsely crushed
    black peppercorns
1 tablespoon sea salt
1 three-bone beef fore rib, about
    375 kg/7¾ lb
1 tablespoon rapeseed oil

## PESTO
25 g/1 oz fresh coriander
25 g/1 oz flat-leaf parsley
4 tablespoons fresh oregano leaves
4 tablespoons hazelnuts, toasted and
    skins removed
4 tablespoons sherry vinegar
3–5 garlic cloves, roughly chopped
½ teaspoon crushed red chilli flakes
120 ml/4 fl oz extra-virgin olive oil

Sea salt
Ground black pepper

2 large handfuls apple or oak wood
    chips, soaked in water for at least
    30 minutes

**1** Mix the peppercorns and salt in a small bowl. Coat the meat on all sides with the oil and season evenly with the peppercorn mixture. Leave the joint to stand at room temperature for 1 hour before grilling.

**2** Process the pesto ingredients, except the oil, in a food processor or blender. Then, with the motor running, slowly add the oil to make a thin paste. Season with salt and pepper. Pour into a serving bowl, cover, and leave to stand at room temperature while cooking the roast.

**3** Prepare the grill for roasting/indirect cooking over medium-low heat (about 180°C/350°F) (see pages 26–27).

**4** Brush the cooking grates clean. Drain and add one handful of the wood chips to the smoker box of a gas grill, following manufacturer's instructions, and close the lid. When smoke appears, cook the meat, bone side down, over **ROASTING/ INDIRECT MEDIUM-LOW HEAT**, with the lid closed, until the internal temperature reaches 49–52°C/120–125°F for medium rare, about 2¼ hours. Drain and add the remaining wood chips to the smoker box after the first hour of cooking.

**5** Remove the joint from the grill and leave to rest for about 20 minutes (the internal temperature will rise 5 to 10 degrees during this time). Cut the meat into thick slices and serve warm with the pesto.

*To toast and skin the hazelnuts, spread the nuts on a baking tray. Bake in a preheated 180°C/350°F/Gas Mark 4 oven for about 10 minutes, stirring occasionally, until the skins are cracked. Transfer to a clean kitchen towel and leave to cool for 10 minutes. Wrap and rub the cooled nuts in the towel to remove the skins (some skin will remain).*

# Pork

# BRINED AND MAPLE-SMOKED BACON

SMOKE INTENSITY: strong

PREP TIME: 15 minutes

BRINING TIME: 48 hours

REFRIGERATION TIME: 12 hours

COOKING TIME: about 3 hours

SPECIAL EQUIPMENT: instant-read meat thermometer

SERVES: 12

## BRINE

3.5 litres/6 pints water
150 g/5 oz sea salt
350 g/11½ oz runny honey
240 ml/8 fl oz maple syrup
1½ teaspoons pink curing salt

2 pieces pork belly, about 2 kg/ 4 lb total weight, rind removed
1 tablespoon black peppercorns, coarsely crushed

9 maple wood chunks

1  Whisk the brine ingredients in a large, non-reactive container until the salt is dissolved. Add the pork bellies and top with a plate to keep them submerged. Cover and refrigerate for 48 hours, no longer.

2  Remove the pork bellies from the container and discard the brine. Rinse the pork under cold running water and pat dry with kitchen paper. Spread the crushed peppercorns on a chopping board and press into the long side of each piece of pork belly. Set the pork bellies on a large wire rack set over a large roasting tray. Refrigerate, uncovered, for 12 hours.

3  Prepare the smoker for roasting/indirect cooking with very low heat (95–130°C/ 200–250°F) (see pages 23–25). When the temperature reaches 110°C/225°F, add three of the wood chunks to the charcoal.

4  Brush the cooking grate clean. Smoke the pork bellies over ROASTING/INDIRECT VERY LOW HEAT for about 3 hours, with the lid closed, until an instant-read meat thermometer inserted into each piece registers 65°C/150°F. Add more lit briquettes as necessary to maintain the heat and add three more wood chunks to the charcoal after the first and second hours. Remove from the smoker and cool completely.

5  Remove any stray bones before using. The bacon can be wrapped in clingfilm and refrigerated for up to 1 week. Or wrap the bacon in plastic and then wrap again in aluminium foil and freeze for up to 3 months.

*If you slice your home-smoked bacon by hand, without a delicatessen-style machine, the slices will be on the thick side (see photo below), so plan on a little extra time when frying them. Or you can simply cut the bacon into chunks for flavouring soups and stews.*

# TERIYAKI PORK BELLY
## WITH CASHEW JASMINE RICE

IDEAL GRILL:

SMOKE INTENSITY: moderate

PREP TIME: 30 minutes

BRAISING TIME: about 3 hours

CHILLING TIME: about 2 hours

REDUCING TIME: 1–1¼ hours

COOKING TIME: about 1½ hours

SPECIAL EQUIPMENT: 5-litre/
8-pint cast-iron casserole,
instant-read meat thermometer

SERVES: 6

*Pork belly is the same cut of pork used for bacon. There are three components to a pork belly, arranged in layers: rind, fat and meat. Choose a pork belly with a good proportion of pink meat compared to the white fat. Like bacon, some of the fat will remain intact when serving the pork belly, so don't expect it to melt away during braising.*

1 Combine the braising liquid ingredients in a 5-litre cast-iron casserole over a high heat, and bring to a simmer, stirring constantly to dissolve the sugar. Place the pork belly in the braising liquid, rind side down, and add more water if needed to barely cover it. Bring to the boil over a high heat and then reduce the heat to low. Cover and simmer for about 3 hours, turning occasionally and adding more water as needed to keep the pork covered, until the pork is very tender when pierced with the tip of a sharp knife. Transfer the pork to a large plate to cool. Reserve the liquid to make the sauce. Cover the pork with clingfilm and refrigerate for about 2 hours until chilled.

2 Set a fine sieve over a large bowl and strain the braising liquid. Discard the solids that remain in the sieve. Leave to stand for 10 minutes. Skim the fat from the surface of the liquid. Rinse the casserole, pour the liquid back into the pan, and bring to the boil over a high heat. Lower the heat and simmer the liquid for 1–1¼ hours until reduced to 240 ml/8 fl oz. Leave to cool. Cover and refrigerate until ready to use.

3 Prepare the smoker for roasting/indirect cooking with very low heat (95–130°C/200–250°F) (see pages 23–25). When the temperature reaches 110°C/225°F, add three of the wood chunks to the charcoal.

4 Brush the cooking grate clean. Smoke the pork belly, rind side up, over ROASTING/INDIRECT VERY LOW HEAT for 1 hour with the lid closed. Then add the remaining wood chunk to the charcoal and continue to smoke the pork for about 30 minutes more until the internal temperature reaches 60°C/140°F. Transfer to a chopping board and leave to rest for about 10 minutes (the internal temperature will rise 5–10 degrees during this time).

5 About 25 minutes before the pork is done, make the rice. Put the rice in a fine sieve and rinse well under cold running water; drain. Bring the rice, water and salt to the boil in a medium saucepan over a high heat. Reduce the heat to medium-low. Cover and simmer for 17–20 minutes until the rice is tender and has absorbed the water. Remove from the heat and add the cashews and spring onions, but do not stir. Cover the saucepan again and leave to stand for 5–10 minutes. Fold in the cashews and spring onions and fluff the rice.

6 Reheat the sauce. Cut the pork crossways into 1-cm/½-inch slices. Spoon the rice into serving bowls, top with slices of pork and drizzle generously with the sauce. Serve warm with any remaining sauce.

## BRAISING LIQUID

1 litre/1¾ pints water

6 spring onions, roughly chopped (white and light green parts only)

120 ml/4 fl oz soy sauce

75 ml/3 fl oz whisky

75 g/3 oz soft light brown sugar

50 g/2 oz fresh ginger, peeled and cut into 1-cm/½-inch slices

3 tablespoons hoisin sauce

2 whole star anise

2 garlic cloves, peeled and crushed

1 pork belly (with rind), about 1.25 kg/2½ lb

4 fist-sized apple or cherry wood chunks

## RICE

300 g/10 oz jasmine rice

350 ml/12 fl oz water

¾ teaspoon sea salt

75 g/3 oz roasted cashews, coarsely chopped

3 spring onions, thinly sliced (white and light green parts only)

# BACON WITH APPLE WOOD SMOKE

IDEAL
GRILL:

SMOKE INTENSITY: strong

PREP TIME: 30 minutes

BRINING TIME: 48 hours

REFRIGERATION TIME: 12 hours

COOKING TIME: 1¾–2 hours

SPECIAL EQUIPMENT: kitchen
string, instant-read meat
thermometer

SERVES: 16

## BRINE

4 tablespoons juniper berries

2 litres/3½ pints water

1 litre/1¾ pints unsweetened
     apple cider

950 ml/1½ lager

150 g/5 oz sea salt

225 g/8 oz soft dark brown sugar,
     preferably muscovado

75 g/3 oz fresh sage

50 g/2 oz fresh thyme sprigs,
     roughly chopped

2 tablespoons pink curing salt
     (sodium nitrate)

1 tablespoon black peppercorns

4 garlic cloves, crushed


1 boneless, centre-cut pork loin
     joint, about 2 kg/4 lb, trimmed of
     excess fat

Vegetable oil

4 apple wood chunks

1 Crush the juniper berries under a heavy saucepan. Transfer them to a very large, non-reactive bowl and mix in the remaining brine ingredients, stirring constantly to dissolve the salt and sugar.

2 Cut the pork in half lengthways, and then tie each half with kitchen string at 5-cm/2-inch intervals to make a compact cylinder. Add the meat to the brine and then place a plate on top to keep it submerged. Cover and refrigerate for 48 hours.

3 Remove the joints from the bowl, and discard the brine. Set on a wire rack on a roasting tray. Refrigerate, uncovered, for 12 hours. The surface of the meat will appear dry. Leave the meat to stand at room temperature for 15–30 minutes before cooking. Brush the joints all over with oil.

4 Prepare the smoker for roasting/indirect cooking with very low heat (95–130°C/ 200–250°F) (see pages 23–25). When the temperature reaches 110°C/225°F, add two wood chunks to the charcoal.

5 Brush the cooking grate clean. Smoke the roasts, fat side up, over ROASTING/ INDIRECT VERY LOW HEAT for 1 hour, with the lid closed, adjusting the vents so the temperature inside the smoker stays as close to 110°C/225°F as possible.

6 Add the remaining wood chunks to the charcoal. Continue smoking over ROASTING/INDIRECT VERY LOW HEAT for 45–60 minutes, with the lid closed, until an instant-read meat thermometer inserted into the centre of each roast registers 65°C/150°F. Remove from the smoker and leave to rest for about 10 minutes. Remove the string and cut the meat crossways into thin slices. Serve warm.

*Pink curing salt (see photo below) is also called sodium nitrate, is usually tinted pink so it isn't confused with regular salt. Pink curing salt is used in charcuterie to discourage bacterial growth and to give the meat an appetizing colour. Do not confuse it with Himalayan and Hawaiian pink salts, which are naturally pink and are considered finishing salts.*

# CEDAR-PLANKED PORK FILLETS
## WITH MANGO AND CURRY

IDEAL
GRILL:

SMOKE INTENSITY: moderate

PREP TIME: 20 minutes

COOKING TIME: 25–30 minutes

SPECIAL EQUIPMENT: 1 untreated
cedar plank, 30–37 cm/
12–15 inches long and about
18 cm/7 inches wide and
1–1.5 cm/½–¾ inch thick, soaked
in water for at least 1 hour;
instant-read meat thermometer

SERVES: 6

*Whenever you are cooking with
a plank, keep it over grilling/
direct heat as long as possible
to generate a good amount of
smoke, but if you see flames
coming from the plank at any
time, move it over roasting/
indirect heat.*

RUB
2 teaspoons curry powder
1 teaspoon dried thyme
1 teaspoon sea salt
½ teaspoon ground black pepper

2 pork fillets, each about 500 g/
    1 lb, trimmed of excess fat and
    silver skin
Vegetable or rapeseed oil

SAUCE
2 ripe mangoes, about 750 g/
    1½ lb total weight, roughly
    chopped
2 tablespoons fresh lime juice
¼ teaspoon curry powder
¼ teaspoon toasted sesame oil
¼ teaspoon sea salt
¼ teaspoon hot pepper sauce

1 tablespoon finely chopped fresh
    coriander (optional)

1 Mix the rub ingredients in a small bowl. Lightly coat the pork fillets on all sides with oil and season evenly with the rub. Leave the meat to stand at room temperature for 15–30 minutes before grilling.

2 Prepare the grill for grilling/direct and roasting/indirect cooking over a medium-high heat (200–230°C/400–450°F) (see pages 26–27).

3 Purée the sauce ingredients in a food processor or blender. If the sauce is too thick, thin with water 1 tablespoon at a time. You should have about 150 ml/¼ pint of sauce.

4 Brush the cooking grates clean. Place the soaked plank over GRILLING/DIRECT MEDIUM-HIGH HEAT and close the lid. After 5–10 minutes, when the plank begins to smoke and char, lay the pork on it and cook over GRILLING/DIRECT MEDIUM-HIGH HEAT for 10 minutes, with the lid closed. Then move the plank over ROASTING/INDIRECT MEDIUM-HIGH HEAT and continue cooking for 15–20 minutes, with the lid closed and turning once, until the internal temperature reaches 63°C/145°F. Remove from the grill and leave to rest for 3–5 minutes.

5 Cut the pork crossways into thick slices, top with the coriander, if liked, and serve with the mango sauce.

# HICKORY PORK FILLETS
## WITH CITRUS-CORIANDER SAUCE

IDEAL
GRILL:

SMOKE INTENSITY: moderate

PREP TIME: 20 minutes

COOKING TIME: about 18 minutes

SPECIAL EQUIPMENT: instant-
read meat thermometer

SERVES: 4

*Add the food to the grill when
the coals reach about 190°C/
375°F, the lower half of the
medium temperature range.
This will allow the pork to be
in contact with the smoke for
a longer period of time and
soak up more smoke flavour.
It will also keep the glaze from
scorching, which is a possibility
at higher temperatures.*

### SAUCE
2 oranges
1 lime
125 g/4 oz granulated sugar
120 ml/4 fl oz whisky
40 g/1½ oz fresh coriander, finely
    chopped

2 pork fillets, each 375–500 g/ 12–16
    oz, trimmed of excess fat and
    silver skin
Extra-virgin olive oil
1 teaspoon sea salt
½ teaspoon crushed red chilli flakes

1 large handful hickory wood chips,
    soaked in water for at least
    30 minutes

1 Finely grate the zest from the oranges and lime and set aside. Juice the oranges (you should have 150 ml/¼ pint juice) and the lime (you should have 3 tablespoons juice). Combine the orange and lime juice and the sugar in a medium, heavy saucepan over a medium-high heat and bring to the boil, stirring just until the sugar is dissolved. Continue cooking, without stirring, until the mixture is covered with large, glossy bubbles and is reduced to about 120 ml/ 4 fl oz. Remove from the heat. Carefully stir in the whisky, taking care that it doesn't ignite. Return the saucepan over medium-high heat and bring to the boil. Cook until syrupy and reduced to 120 ml/4 fl oz, stirring occasionally. Pour into a heatproof container and allow to cool. Stir in the coriander, orange and lime zest.

2 Lightly brush the pork fillets with oil and season evenly with the salt and red chilli flakes.

3 Prepare a two-zone fire for medium heat (180–230°C/350–450°F) (see pages 20–22).

4 Brush the cooking grate clean. Drain and add the wood chips to the charcoal and put the lid on the grill. When the wood begins to smoke, cook the pork over GRILLING/DIRECT MEDIUM HEAT for about 10 minutes, with the lid closed as much as possible and turning occasionally, until the outsides are seared and golden brown. Then generously brush the tops with some of the sauce, close the lid, and cook for 3 minutes. Turn the pork over and brush with more sauce. Close the lid and cook for about 5 minutes more, until the internal temperature reaches 63°C/145°F. Remove from the grill and leave to rest for 3–5 minutes. Cut the fillets across into 1-cm/½-inch slices and serve with the remaining sauce.

# WOOD-SMOKED PORK TACOS
## WITH BLACK BEAN SALSA

IDEAL GRILL:

SMOKE INTENSITY: mild

PREP TIME: 30 minutes

COOKING TIME: 30–35 minutes

SPECIAL EQUIPMENT: instant-read meat thermometer, large disposable foil tray

SERVES: 4–6

*Don't be tempted to cook the pork directly over the coals. Slower cooking ensures a smokier flavour.*

### SALSA
475-g/15-oz can black beans, rinsed
200 g/7 oz tomatoes, finely chopped
200 g/7 oz tomatillos (Mexican green tomatoes), or tomatoes if unavailable, finely chopped
2 tablespoons finely chopped fresh coriander
2 tablespoons extra-virgin olive oil
1 tablespoon fresh lime juice
1 tablespoon finely chopped serrano chilli
1 teaspoon finely chopped garlic

Sea salt
Ground black pepper

### RUB
½ teaspoon prepared chilli seasoning
½ teaspoon ground cumin
¼ teaspoon garlic granules

1 pork fillet, about 500 g/1 lb, trimmed of excess fat and silver skin
Extra-virgin olive oil
2 large handfuls mesquite wood chips, soaked in water for at least 30 minutes
12 corn tortillas (15 cm/6 inches)
Ready-made guacamole

1 Combine the salsa ingredients in a medium, non-reactive bowl. Season with salt and pepper. Mix gently but thoroughly. If liked, to fully incorporate the flavours, leave the salsa to sit at room temperature for up to 1 hour in a covered bowl.

2 Prepare a two-zone fire for high heat (230–290°C/450–550°F) (see pages 20–22).

3 Mix the rub ingredients, including ½ teaspoon salt and ¼ teaspoon pepper in a small bowl. Lightly brush the pork all over with oil and season evenly with the rub. Set aside at room temperature for 15–30 minutes before cooking.

4 Brush the cooking grate clean. Drain and add the wood chips to the charcoal and put the lid on the grill. When the wood begins to smoke, cook the pork over ROASTING/INDIRECT HIGH HEAT for 20–25 minutes, with the lid closed as much as possible, until the internal temperature reaches 63°C/145°F. Remove from the grill and wrap with aluminium foil. Leave to rest for about 15 minutes or until cool enough to handle.

5 Cut the meat across into six pieces. Shred and transfer to a large disposable foil tray. Add the salsa and mix well. About 15 minutes before you are ready to serve, warm the pork and black bean salsa over ROASTING/INDIRECT LOW OR MEDIUM HEAT for about 10 minutes. Meanwhile, brush one side of each tortilla with oil and lightly season with salt. Grill the tortillas, oil side down, over grilling/direct heat for about 1 minute (do not turn). Divide the pork and salsa between the tortillas and serve with guacamole.

# CHILLI-RUBBED PORK CHOPS
## WITH SMOKED TOMATILLO SAUCE

**IDEAL GRILL:**

**SMOKE INTENSITY:** moderate

**PREP TIME:** 25 minutes

**MARINATING TIME:** 20–30 minutes

**COOKING TIME:** 8–10 minutes

**SPECIAL EQUIPMENT:** perforated grill pan

**SERVES:** 4

### RUB

2 teaspoons chilli powder
2 teaspoons garlic powder
1 teaspoon ground cumin

Sea salt
Ground black pepper

4 bone-in pork loin chops, each about 8 oz and 2.5 cm/1 inch thick, trimmed of excess fat
Extra-virgin olive oil

4 tomatillos (Mexican green tomatoes), about 275 g/9 oz total weight, papery husks removed, or regular tomatoes if unavailable, rinsed, cut in half
2 slices onion, each about 5 mm/¼ inch thick
1 large jalapeño chilli pepper, about 40 g/1½ oz, halved lengthways, seeds removed

2 large handfuls mesquite wood chips, soaked in water for at least 30 minutes

40 g/1½ oz fresh coriander, roughly chopped
½ teaspoon soft light brown sugar

*A jalapeño chilli pepper gives the sauce a kick, and removing the seeds makes it milder. For extra zip, add the seeds or toss in another jalapeño.*

1 Mix the rub ingredients, including 1 teaspoon salt and ½ teaspoon pepper in a small bowl. Lightly brush the pork chops on both sides with oil and season evenly with the rub. Cover and marinate at room temperature for 20–30 minutes.

2 Prepare a two-zone fire for medium heat (180–230°C/350–450°F) (see pages 20–22) and preheat the grill pan on the cooking grate.

3 Lightly brush the tomatillos, onion and jalapeño with oil.

4 Brush the cooking grate clean. Drain and add the wood chips to the charcoal and put the lid on the grill. When the wood begins to smoke, arrange the vegetables in a single layer on the grill pan and place the chops on the cooking grate. Cook over **GRILLING/DIRECT MEDIUM HEAT** for 8–10 minutes, with the lid closed as much as possible and turning once or twice, until the vegetables are crisp-tender and the chops are still slightly pink in the centre. Remove the vegetables and chops from the grill and leave the chops to rest for 3–5 minutes.

5 Cut the vegetables into bite-sized pieces and place in a bowl. Add the coriander and brown sugar and toss to combine. Season with salt and pepper. Serve the pork chops warm with the tomatillo sauce.

# BEST-ON-THE-BLOCK BABY BACK RIBS

**IDEAL GRILL:**

**SMOKE INTENSITY:** moderate

**PREP TIME:** 30 minutes

**COOKING TIME:** about 3 hours

**SPECIAL EQUIPMENT:** rib rack, small spray bottle

**SERVES:** 6–8

## RUB

2 tablespoons sea salt
1 tablespoon smoked paprika
1 tablespoon garlic granules
1 tablespoon chilli powder
2 teaspoons mustard powder
2 teaspoons dried thyme
1 teaspoon ground cumin
1 teaspoon celery seeds
1 teaspoon ground black pepper

4 racks baby back ribs, each 1.25–
    1.5 kg/2½–3 lb

4 large handfuls hickory wood chips,
    soaked in water for at least
    30 minutes

## SAUCE

4 bacon rashers
240 ml/8 fl oz tomato ketchup
120 ml/4 fl oz unsweetened
    apple juice
4 tablespoons cider vinegar
1 tablespoon black treacle
2 teaspoons Worcestershire sauce
½ teaspoon smoked paprika
½ teaspoon ground cumin
¼ teaspoon sea salt
¼ teaspoon ground black pepper
Hot pepper sauce (optional)

## MOP

120 ml/4 fl oz unsweetened apple
    juice
1 tablespoon cider vinegar

*These ribs are at their tender best when slow cooked with low roasting/indirect heat from all sides. Cooking them on a big, six-burner gas grill (equipped with a smoker box) will allow you to arrange all four racks in the centre of the cooking grates, without any of them hanging over the direct heat from the outside burners. If you are using a smaller grill, it would be wise to cook just two or three racks.*

1 Mix the rub ingredients in a small bowl. Using a round-bladed knife, slide the tip under the membrane covering the back of each rack of ribs. Lift and loosen the membrane until it breaks, then grab a corner of it with some kitchen paper and pull it off. Season the racks evenly with the rub. Arrange the racks in the rib rack, standing each rack up and facing in the same direction. Leave the racks to stand at room temperature for 30–60 minutes before cooking.

2 Prepare the grill for roasting/indirect cooking over low heat (150–180°C/300–350°F) (see pages 26–27).

3 Brush the cooking grates clean. Drain and add two handfuls of the wood chips to the smoker box of a gas grill, following manufacturer's instructions, and close the lid. When the wood begins to smoke, cook the racks over ROASTING/INDIRECT LOW HEAT for 1 hour, with the lid closed. Maintain the temperature of the grill between 150 and 180°C/300 and 350°F.

4 Cook the bacon for 10–15 minutes in a medium frying pan over low heat, turning occasionally, until brown and crispy. Drain the bacon on kitchen paper and eat the bacon whenever you like, but reserve the bacon fat in the frying pan and leave it to cool to room temperature. Combine all the remaining sauce ingredients, except the hot pepper sauce, in a medium saucepan. Add 3 tablespoons of the bacon fat, whisk until smooth and cook over low heat for about 5 minutes. If you like a spicy sauce, season with hot pepper sauce. Remove the saucepan from the heat.

5 Combine the mop ingredients in a small spray bottle or bowl. After the first hour of cooking, drain and add the remaining wood chips to the smoker box. Lightly spray or brush the racks with the mop, particularly the areas that are looking a little dry. Close the lid and cook for a second hour. Maintain the temperature of the grill between 150 and 180°C/300 and 350°F.

6 After the second hour of cooking, lightly spray or brush the racks with the mop, particularly the areas that are looking a little dry. If any racks are cooking faster than the others or look much darker, swap their positions for even cooking. Cook for another 30 minutes or so.

7 After 2½ hours, the meat will have shrunk back from most of the bones by 5 mm/¼ inch or more. If it has not, continue to cook until it does. Remove the racks in the rib rack from the grill. Close the lid of the grill to maintain the heat. Remove the racks from the rib rack and brush each on both sides with sauce.

8 Return the racks to the grill over ROASTING/INDIRECT LOW HEAT. At this point you can pile all the racks on top of one another or stack the racks in twos. Continue to cook over ROASTING/INDIRECT LOW HEAT for 15–30 minutes, with the lid closed, until tender and succulent. They are done when you lift a rack at one end with tongs, bone side up, and the rack bends so much in the middle that the meat tears easily. If the meat does not tear easily, continue to cook until it does. Just before serving, lightly brush the racks with sauce again. Cut the racks into individual ribs and serve warm.

# CHAMPIONSHIP SPARERIBS
## WITH SWEET APPLE BARBECUE SAUCE

IDEAL
GRILL:

SMOKE INTENSITY: strong

PREP TIME: 45 minutes

COOKING TIME: 4¾–6 hours

SPECIAL EQUIPMENT: small
spray bottle

SERVES: 8

### RUB
3 tablespoons sea salt
2 tablespoons ancho chilli powder
2 tablespoons soft light brown sugar
2 tablespoons garlic granules
1 tablespoon ground cumin
2 teaspoons ground black pepper

4 racks spareribs, each 1.25–1.5
    kg/2½–3½ lb

175 ml/6 fl oz unsweetened apple
    juice
4 tablespoons cider vinegar

5 fist-sized hickory wood chunks

### SAUCE
475 ml/16 fl oz tomato ketchup
120 ml/4 fl oz unsweetened apple
    juice
4 tablespoons cider vinegar
4 tablespoons prepared mustard
2 tablespoons black treacle
2 tablespoons Worcestershire sauce
1 teaspoon garlic granules
¼ teaspoon chipotle chilli powder

*A great rack of ribs should have a layer of bark, that is, a dark brown and well-seasoned crust. Before you wrap the ribs in foil, make sure the bark is dark.*

1  Prepare the smoker for roasting/indirect cooking with very low heat (110–130°C/225–250°F) (see pages 23–25).

2  Mix the rub ingredients in a medium bowl. Put the spareribs, meaty side up, on a chopping board. Follow the line of fat that separates the meaty ribs from the much tougher tips at the base of each rack, and cut off the tips. Turn each rack over. Cut off the flap of meat attached to the centre of each rack. Also cut off the flap of meat that hangs below the shorter end of the ribs. Using a rounded knife, slide the tip under the membrane covering the back of each rack of ribs. Lift and loosen the membrane until it breaks, then grab a corner of it with a piece of kitchen paper and pull it off. Season the spareribs all over with the rub, putting more of the rub on the meaty sides than on the bone sides.

3  Combine 175 ml/6 fl oz apple juice and 4 tablespoons cider vinegar in a small spray bottle.

4  Brush the cooking grate clean. Add two of the wood chunks to the charcoal. Smoke the spareribs, bone side down, over ROASTING/INDIRECT VERY LOW HEAT for 4–5 hours, with the lid closed, until the meat has shrunk back from the bones at least 1 cm/½ inch. After each hour, add more lit briquettes as necessary to maintain the heat, add one more wood chunk to the charcoal (until they are gone) and spray the ribs on both sides with the apple juice mixture. Meanwhile, make the sauce.

5  Combine the sauce ingredients in a medium saucepan over a medium heat and bring to a simmer. Reduce the heat to low and cook for 15–20 minutes, stirring occasionally.

6  When the spareribs are done, remove them from the smoker. Brush the racks on both sides with the sauce and wrap each rack in heavy-duty aluminium foil. Return the foil-wrapped racks to the smoker, stacking them on the top cooking grate. Continue to cook over ROASTING/INDIRECT VERY LOW HEAT for 45–60 minutes, with the lid closed, until the meat is tender enough to tear with your fingers. Remove the spareribs from the smoker and lightly brush the racks on both sides with sauce again. Cut the racks into individual ribs. Serve warm with the remaining sauce on the side.

# PACIFIC RIM PORK ROAST
## WITH MANGO SALSA

**IDEAL GRILL:**

**SMOKE INTENSITY:** strong

**PREP TIME:** 30 minutes

**COOKING TIME:** 8–10 hours

**SPECIAL EQUIPMENT:** spice mill, instant-read meat thermometer

**SERVES:** 8–10

1 bone-in pork shoulder joint
    3.5–4 kg/7–8 lb
5 teaspoons Hawaiian red salt
2 teaspoons Sichuan peppercorns
1 teaspoon black peppercorns

**MOP**
175 ml/6 fl oz pineapple juice,
    preferably chilled rather
    than canned
2 tablespoons wholegrain mustard
2 tablespoons cider vinegar

4 fist-sized apple wood chunks

**SALSA**
4 mangoes, about 1 kg/2 lb total
    weight, cut into 5-mm/¼-inch
    pieces
2 spring onions (white and light
    green parts only), finely chopped
3 tablespoons fresh lime juice
2 tablespoons finely chopped fresh
    Thai basil or mint leaves
1 tablespoon Thai fish sauce
1 tablespoon peeled, finely chopped
    fresh ginger
1 small bird's eye *or* serrano chilli,
    deseeded and finely chopped

2 heads round lettuce, separated
    into leaves

1 Using a very sharp knife, trim the pork's exterior fat so that it is no thicker than 5 mm/¼ inch. Whirl the salt and the peppercorns in a spice mill until finely ground. Rub the mixture all over the meat and leave to stand at room temperature for 1 hour before grilling.

2 Whisk the mop ingredients in a small, non-reactive bowl and set aside.

3 Prepare the smoker for roasting/indirect cooking with very low heat (95–130°C/200–250°F) (see pages 23–25). When the temperature reaches 110°C/225°F, add two wood chunks to the charcoal.

4 Brush the cooking grate clean. Smoke the pork, fat side up, over **ROASTING/INDIRECT VERY LOW HEAT** for 8–10 hours, with the lid closed and turning once after 4 hours, until the internal temperature registers 88°C/190°F. Add one more wood chunk after the first and second hours and brush both sides of the meat with the mop every hour. Maintain the temperature of the smoker between 110 and 130°C/225 and 250°F by adjusting the vents and adding more lit briquettes as necessary. Transfer the pork to a plate, loosely cover with foil, and leave to rest for about 30 minutes. Meanwhile, make the salsa.

5 Mix the salsa ingredients in a large, non-reactive bowl. Cover and refrigerate until serving.

6 Using two forks or your fingers, pull the pork apart into shreds, discarding any pockets of fat. Pile the pulled pork on to individual lettuce leaves and top with the mango salsa. Serve warm or at room temperature.

*Hawaiian red salt has a complex mineral flavour and is available at some supermarkets and delicatessens and online.*

# QUINTESSENTIAL PULLED PORK SANDWICHES

**IDEAL GRILL:**

**SMOKE INTENSITY:** strong

**PREP TIME:** 30 minutes

**COOKING TIME:** 8-10 hours

**RESTING TIME:** 1 hour

**SPECIAL EQUIPMENT:** food syringe, instant-read meat thermometer

**SERVES:** 12

1 bone-in pork shoulder joint
    3.5–4 kg/7–8 lb

120 ml/4 fl oz unsweetened apple juice
Sea salt
1 tablespoon soft light brown sugar
1 tablespoon Worcestershire sauce

### RUB

1 tablespoon soft light brown sugar
2 teaspoons paprika
1 teaspoon prepared chilli seasoning
1 teaspoon garlic granules
1 teaspoon mustard powder
1 teaspoon ground black pepper

10 fist-sized hickory wood chunks

### SAUCE

350 ml/12 fl oz tomato ketchup
175 ml/6 fl oz unsweetened apple juice
175 ml/6 fl oz cider vinegar
3 tablespoons soft light brown sugar
3 tablespoons tomato purée
1½ tablespoons black treacle
1 tablespoon Worcestershire sauce
1½ teaspoons mustard powder
¾ teaspoon hot pepper sauce
½ teaspoon ground black pepper

12 hamburger buns
200 g/7 oz cups ready-made or home-made coleslaw

*Patience. A pork shoulder can be a tough cut of meat. It takes time to break down the muscle fibres and to melt the connective tissues. So get yourself a reliable thermometer and wait as long as it takes for your pork shoulder to reach 88°C/190°F before you try to pull or shred the meat. This recipe is worth every minute it requires.*

1 Using a very sharp knife, trim the pork's exterior fat so that it is no thicker than 5 mm/¼ inch. Whisk the apple juice, 2 tablespoons salt, brown sugar, Worcestershire sauce and 4 tablespoons water in a small bowl until the salt and sugar have dissolved. Inject the meat with the liquid flavouring: With the fat side facing down, imagine the joint in 2.5-cm/1-inch squares and, using a food syringe, inject each square with some of the liquid, slowly pulling the needle out as you inject the liquid. Some liquid will seep out, but try to keep as much as possible inside the meat.

2 Mix the rub ingredients including 2 teaspoons salt in a small bowl. Coat the surface of the meat evenly with the rub. Leave the pork to stand at room temperature for 30 minutes before cooking.

3 Prepare the smoker for roasting/indirect cooking with very low heat (95–130°C/ 200–250°F) (see pages 22–25). When the temperature reaches 110°C/225°F, add two wood chunks to the charcoal.

4 Brush the cooking grate clean. Smoke the pork, fat side up, over ROASTING/INDIRECT VERY LOW HEAT for 5 hours, with the lid closed, adjusting the vents so the temperature of the smoker stays as close to 110°C/225°F as possible. At the start of every hour (after the first hour), add two more wood chunks to the charcoal. If the temperature falls below 95°C/200°F and can't be raised by adjusting the vents, add more lit briquettes as needed.

5 After 5 hours, use an instant-read meat thermometer to check the internal temperature of the meat. If it has not reached 70°C/160°F, continue cooking until it does. If it has reached 70°C/160°F, remove the meat from the smoker. Put the lid back on the smoker to prevent heat loss. Add more lit briquettes and refill the water pan to maintain the 110°C/225°F temperature.

6 On a large work surface, lay out two sheets of heavy-duty aluminium foil, each about 90 cm/3 feet long, overlapping the sheets slightly along their longer sides. Place the pork in the centre of the foil, fat side up. Fold up the edges to wrap the meat tightly to trap the steam. Return the pork to the smoker and cook over ROASTING/INDIRECT VERY LOW HEAT for at least 3 hours and as long as 5 hours, with the lid closed, until the internal temperature reaches 88°C/190°F. Remove from the smoker and leave to rest, in the foil, for 1 hour.

7 Whisk the sauce ingredients, including ¾ teaspoon salt, in a medium, heavy saucepan. Bring to a simmer over a medium heat and cook for about 5 minutes, stirring occasionally. Set aside.

8 Unwrap the pork and, when cool enough to handle, pull the meat apart to shred it. Discard any large pieces of fat and sinew. Moisten the pork with plenty of sauce and cook in a large saucepan over a low heat, until warmed through, stirring occasionally. Pile the pulled pork on buns and top with coleslaw, such as Sweet and Tangy Vegetable Slaw (see page 196). Serve with additional sauce.

# SLOW-ROASTED HAM
## WITH SWEET-AND-SOUR CIDER GLAZE

**IDEAL GRILL:**

**SMOKE INTENSITY:** strong

**PREP TIME:** 15 minutes

**COOKING TIME:** 1¼–2 hours

**SPECIAL EQUIPMENT:** large disposable foil tray, instant-read meat thermometer

**SERVES:** 10–12

1 whole, fully cooked, bone-in
    smoked ham, 4–5 kg/8–10 lb

4 large handfuls apple wood chips,
    soaked in water for at least
    30 minutes

### GLAZE
120 ml/4 fl oz cider vinegar
120 ml/4 fl oz tomato ketchup
4 tablespoons fresh lime juice
3 tablespoons soft dark brown sugar
2 tablespoons soy sauce
1 tablespoon Dijon mustard
½ teaspoon ground black pepper

*To prevent the ham from drying out, keep some water in the roasting tray at all times. Whenever you add more briquettes to the fire, check to see if the tray needs another 6 tablespoons or so.*

1 Leave the ham to stand at room temperature for about 30 minutes before cooking.

2 Prepare a two-zone fire for low heat (130–180°C/250–350°F) (see pages 20–22).

3 Brush the cooking grate clean. Drain and add two handfuls of the wood chips to the charcoal and put the lid on the grill. Put the ham, flat side down, in a large disposable foil tray and add water. When the wood begins to smoke, place the tray on the cooking grate over ROASTING/INDIRECT LOW HEAT. Cook the ham for 1¼–2 hours (about 10 minutes per 500 g/lb), with the lid closed as much as possible, until an instant-read meat thermometer inserted into the thickest part of the ham (not touching the bone) reaches 60°C/135°F. Replenish the charcoal as needed to maintain a steady temperature, adding three to five lit briquettes to each pile every 45 minutes, along with the remaining drained wood chips. Meanwhile, make the glaze.

4 Combine the glaze ingredients in a small saucepan and simmer over a medium heat for 3–4 minutes until heated through. Remove from the heat.

5 Glaze the ham during the last 30 minutes of cooking time. If the meat begins to look too dark, cover it with foil and stop glazing. Carefully transfer the ham from the foil tray to a chopping board. Tent with foil and leave to rest for 15–20 minutes. Cut the ham into slices and serve warm.

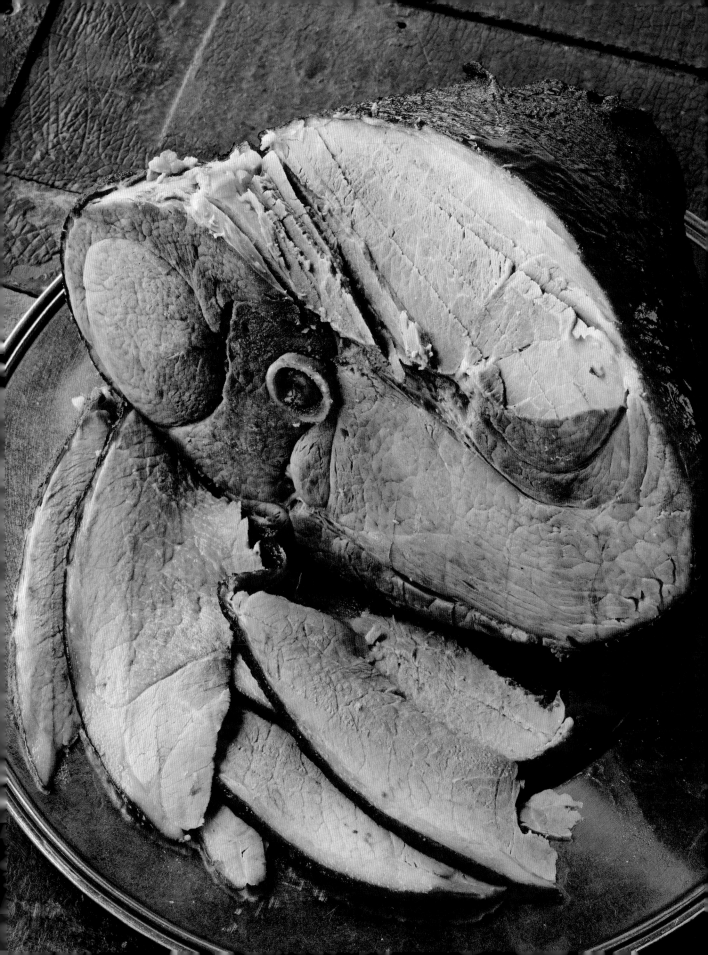

# SAGE-SMOKED FRESH HAM
## BASTED WITH MAPLE SYRUP

IDEAL GRILL:

**SMOKE INTENSITY:** strong

**PREP TIME:** 30 minutes

**COOKING TIME:** about 5½ hours

**SPECIAL EQUIPMENT:** large disposable foil tray, kitchen string, instant-read thermometer

**SERVES:** 14

### RUB
25 g/1 oz fresh sage sprigs
1 tablespoon sea salt
1 teaspoon ground black pepper

½ fresh ham, preferably the leg end, about 4–4 kg/9 lb, rind removed (if attached), and fat trimmed to a thin layer
1 tablespoon vegetable oil

5 large handfuls apple wood chips (1 handful left dry; 4 handfuls soaked in water for at least 30 minutes)

120 ml/4 fl oz maple syrup

1 Remove and roughly chop enough sage leaves from the sprigs to measure 2 tablespoons. Add the salt and pepper and chop until the sage is very finely chopped. Scrape into a small bowl. Reserve the remaining sage sprigs.

2 Making cuts about 2.5 cm/1 inch apart, lightly score the ham fat with a thin, sharp knife. Tie a few loops of kitchen string around the circumference of the ham to help keep its shape during cooking. Brush the ham with the oil and season with the rub, pressing the spices into the meat. Leave the ham to stand at room temperature for 15–30 minutes before cooking.

3 Carefully place a large disposable foil tray underneath the cooking grates to catch the drippings. Prepare the grill for roasting/indirect cooking over low heat (130–180°C/250–350°F) (see pages 26–27). Place the dry wood chips in the smoker box of a gas grill, following manufacturer's instructions, and let them ignite and smoulder.

4 Brush the cooking grates clean. Drain and add a handful of wood chips to the smouldering chips in the smoker box. Centre the ham over the foil tray and cook over ROASTING/INDIRECT LOW HEAT for 4 hours, with the lid closed. Keep the grill temperature as close to 170°C/325°F as possible. After every hour, add another handful of drained wood chips to the smoker box.

5 After 4 hours, place half the sage sprigs and the final addition of drained wood chips into the smoker box. Baste the ham with half the syrup. Close the lid and continue cooking over ROASTING/INDIRECT LOW HEAT for 30 minutes.

6 Baste the ham with the remaining syrup and add the remaining sage sprigs to the smoker box. Continue cooking for about 1 hour more until an instant-read meat thermometer inserted into the centre of the ham (not touching the bone) registers 70°C/160°F. During the last 15 minutes, increase the temperature of the grill to medium heat (180–230°C/350–450°F) to deepen the colour of the glaze. Transfer the ham to a chopping board and leave to rest for about 15 minutes. Cut the ham into thin slices and serve warm.

# APPLE-BRINED PORK LOIN

## WITH CRANBERRY SAUCE

IDEAL GRILL:

SMOKE INTENSITY: strong

PREP TIME: 20 minutes

BRINING TIME: 4–5 hours

COOKING TIME: 3½–4 hours

SPECIAL EQUIPMENT: instant-read meat thermometer

SERVES: 8

### BRINE

2 lemons

2 litres/3½ pints chilled unsweetened apple juice

8 tablespoons sea salt

120 ml/4 fl oz soy sauce

75 g/3 oz fresh ginger, peeled and thinly sliced

1 tablespoon dried rosemary

1 teaspoon black peppercorns

2 bay leaves

1 bone-in pork loin, about 2.25 kg/ 4½ lb

6 fist-sized apple or hickory wood chunks

### SAUCE

375 g/12 oz fresh or frozen cranberries

225 g/8 oz runny honey

120 ml/4 fl oz unsweetened apple juice or fresh orange juice or water

1 Granny Smith apple, peeled, cored, and cut into 1-cm/½-inch pieces

3 tablespoons calvados

*Make sure the butcher removes the chine bone, the thick piece of the backbone attached to the ribs. This will allow you to cut the roast between the bones into individual chops.*

1 Use a vegetable peeler to remove the zest in wide strips from the lemons. Put the zest in a medium saucepan with half the apple juice, the salt, soy sauce, ginger, rosemary, peppercorns and bay leaves. Bring to a simmer to release their flavours, stirring occasionally. Pour into a non-reactive, heatproof bowl set in a larger bowl of iced water. Allow to stand for about 30 minutes until chilled, stirring often. Stir the remaining chilled apple juice into the brine.

2 Put the joint in the brine, cover and refrigerate for 4–5 hours. Remove the meat from the brine and rinse under cold water. Pat dry with kitchen paper. Leave the roast to stand at room temperature for about 30 minutes before cooking.

3 Prepare the smoker for roasting/indirect cooking with very low heat (95–130°C/ 200–250°F) (see pages 23–25). When the temperature reaches 110°C/225°F, add three wood chunks to the charcoal.

4 Brush the cooking grate clean. Smoke the roast over ROASTING/INDIRECT VERY LOW HEAT for 3½–4 hours, with the lid closed as much as possible, until the internal temperature reaches 65°C/150°F, adding the remaining three wood chunks after the first hour and additional lit briquettes as necessary to maintain the temperature inside the smoker. Remove the pork from the smoker and leave to rest for about 10 minutes (the internal temperature will rise 5–10 degrees during this time). While the pork rests, make the sauce.

5 Combine the cranberries, honey and apple juice in a medium saucepan over a medium-high heat, and bring to a simmer. Reduce the heat to medium and cook for about 7 minutes, stirring often, until the juices are syrupy. Stir in the apple and the calvados. Cook for about 5 minutes, stirring often, until the apple is crisp-tender. The sauce can be served warm or at room temperature. (The sauce will thicken as it cools.)

6 Cut the pork between the bones into individual chops. Serve warm with the sauce.

# SMOKED ROSEMARY PORK LOIN
## WITH CREAMY SAUERKRAUT

IDEAL GRILL:

SMOKE INTENSITY: moderate

PREP TIME: 20 minutes

MARINATING TIME: 30 minutes

COOKING TIME: 1¼–1½ hours

SPECIAL EQUIPMENT: instant-read meat thermometer

SERVES: 4

### MARINADE

3 tablespoons extra-virgin olive oil

2 tablespoons dry white wine

2 tablespoons finely chopped fresh rosemary leaves

1 tablespoon finely chopped fresh thyme leaves

1 teaspoon sea salt

½ teaspoon ground black pepper

1 bone-in pork loin, about 1.5 kg/3 lb

4 large handfuls hickory or oak wood chips, soaked in water for at least 30 minutes

### SAUERKRAUT

2 bacon rashers, finely chopped

1 onion, finely chopped

475 g/15 oz bottled or canned sauerkraut, rinsed

240 ml/8 fl oz chicken stock

120 ml/4 fl oz dry white wine

5 tablespoons heavy whipping cream

Sea salt

Ground black pepper

Freshly grated nutmeg

Boiled new potatoes (optional)

*When purchasing the pork, make sure to get a joint with at least four bones so that each person will have a nice thick pork chop with a rib bone attached. Ask the butcher to remove the chine bone (backbone) so that after the roast is cooked, you can cut between the rib bones easily.*

1 Whisk the marinade ingredients in a medium bowl. Spread about half of the marinade all over the joint. Reserve the remaining marinade for basting later. Allow the meat to marinate at room temperature for 30 minutes before cooking.

2 Prepare the grill for roasting/indirect cooking over medium heat (180–230°C/ 350–450°F).

3 Brush the cooking grates clean. Drain and add two handfuls of the wood chips to the smoker box of a gas grill, following manufacturer's instructions, and close the lid. When smoke begins to pour out of the grill, cook the pork, bone side down, over ROASTING/INDIRECT MEDIUM HEAT for 30 minutes, with the lid closed. Keep the temperature of the grill as close to 180°C/350°F as possible.

4 After 30 minutes baste the meat with the reserved marinade and drain and add the remaining wood chips to the smoker box. Continue to cook for 45–60 minutes more, with the lid closed, until the internal temperature reaches 65°C/150°F. While the meat is cooking, prepare the sauerkraut.

5 Brown the bacon for 4–6 minutes in a medium saucepan over a medium heat, stirring occasionally. Remove the bacon from the saucepan. Add the onion to the pan and cook for 4–6 minutes, stirring occasionally, until tender. Add the sauerkraut, stock, wine and cream and season with salt, pepper and nutmeg. Simmer for 15–20 minutes until most of the liquid has evaporated and the sauerkraut reaches your desired consistency. Remove the saucepan from the heat. Stir in the bacon.

6 When the pork is done, transfer it to a chopping board and leave it to rest for 10–15 minutes (the internal temperature will rise 5–10 degrees during this time). Warm the sauerkraut over medium heat. Cut the joint between the bones. Serve the pork chops warm with sauerkraut and boiled new potatoes, if liked.

# 5

# Poultry

# SMOKED DUCK AND CHERRY SAUSAGES

IDEAL GRILL:

SMOKE INTENSITY: mild

PREP TIME: 1½ hours

FREEZING TIME: 3 hours

REFRIGERATION TIME: 24 hours

COOKING TIME: about 25 minutes

SPECIAL EQUIPMENT: meat mincer, sausage stuffing equipment, instant-read meat thermometer

SERVES: 6–8 (makes 12 sausages, each about 12 cm/5 inches long)

1 kg/2 lb boneless, skinless duck
    meat, cut into 2.5-cm/1-inch
    chunks (from 2 whole 2.5-kg/
    5-lb ducks or 8 duck breasts or
    2 kg/4 lb duck leg quarters)
375 g/12 oz pork belly, rind removed,
    cut into 2.5-cm/1-inch chunks

75 g/3 oz dried tart cherries,
    roughly chopped
4 tablespoons tawny port, chilled
4 tablespoons ice-cold water
2½ teaspoons sea salt
2½ teaspoons ground black pepper
1 teaspoon paprika
1 garlic clove, finely chopped
½ teaspoon dried thyme
½ teaspoon dried sage
½ teaspoon pink curing salt
    (sodium nitrate)
¼ teaspoon ground allspice

120 cm/4 feet prepared sausage
    casings, soaked in cold water for
    30 minutes
Vegetable oil
1 large handful hickory wood chips,
    soaked in water for at least
    30 minutes

*Cold temperature is the key to making sausage. If the meat gets warm at any point in the procedure, the fat softens and makes the sausage greasy. For this reason, the meat is frozen before mincing, the port and water are ice cold, and the sausage mixture sits in a bowl of ice while awaiting stuffing.*

1 Spread the chunks of duck and pork belly on a large roasting tray. Freeze for about 2 hours until frosty but not hard. Remove from the freezer and mince the meat through the coarse blade of a meat mincer, or through the mincing attachment of an electric mixer, into a large, non-reactive bowl. Freeze for 1 hour.

2 Add the dried cherries, port, water, sea salt, pepper, paprika, garlic, thyme, sage, pink curing salt and allspice to the chilled minced meat. Mix well with a large spoon. Place the bowl in a larger bowl of iced water to keep it cold throughout the stuffing process.

3 Rinse the casings several times by running cold water inside the entire length of the casing. Attach the sausage stuffing equipment to an electric mixer according to manufacturer's instructions. Lubricate the tip of the stuffer tube with oil and slide the casing on to the stuffer tube. Tie the end of the casing. Push the meat mixture through the stuffer tube, forcing it into the casing. After you have a 12-cm/5-inch sausage, twist the casing a couple of times and then create another sausage. Keep going until all the meat is used. You will be able to make about 12 sausages. Knot the open end of the casing. Roll the sausage rope into a spiral and place it on a roasting tray. Cover with clingfilm and refrigerate for 24 hours to blend the flavours.

4 Prepare a two-zone fire for medium heat (180–230°C/350–450°F) (see pages 20–22).

5 Pierce each sausage a few times with the tip of a skewer or once with a fork. Brush the cooking grate clean. Drain and add the wood chips to the charcoal and put the lid on the grill. When smoke appears, cook the sausage coil over ROASTING/INDIRECT MEDIUM HEAT for about 25 minutes, with the lid closed, until an instant-read meat thermometer inserted into the centre of one sausage reaches 74°C/165°F. Remove from the grill and cut into individual sausages. Serve immediately.

*If you want to skip the stuffing process altogether, shape the sausage mixture into eight patties, each about 12 cm/5 inches in diameter. Lightly brush the patties with oil. Cook over* **ROASTING/INDIRECT MEDIUM HEAT** *for about 20 minutes (do not turn), with the lid closed, until firm. Then move over* **DIRECT MEDIUM HEAT** *and cook for about 3 minutes, turning once, until lightly browned on both sides. The patties are great on their own, but they also make excellent burgers.*

# TEA-SMOKED DUCK BREASTS
## WITH SWEET SOY DIPPING SAUCE

**IDEAL GRILL:**

**SMOKE INTENSITY:** moderate

**PREP TIME:** 15 minutes

**COOKING TIME:** 10–11 minutes

**SPECIAL EQUIPMENT:** large disposable foil tray, 30-cm/ 12-inch cast-iron frying pan

**SERVES:** 4

*Like wood chips, dried tea and brown sugar release aromatic smoke, but by themselves they tend to burn out quickly. Adding rice to the mixture extends the length of time for the tea and sugar to smoulder.*

### RUB
1½ teaspoons Chinese five spice
1½ teaspoons garlic powder
½ teaspoon sea salt

duck breast halves, each 125–175 g/ 4–6 oz

4 tablespoons loose-leaf black tea
3 tablespoons soft light brown sugar
50 g/2 oz white rice (short or long grain)

### SAUCE
75 g/3 fl oz fresh lemon juice
4 tablespoons soy sauce
2 tablespoons runny honey

1 Prepare a two-zone fire for medium heat (180–230°C/350–450°F) (see pages 20–22). Place a large disposable foil tray beside the bed of charcoal and fill three-quarters full with water.

2 Mix the rub ingredients in a small bowl. Using a sharp knife, score the skin of each duck breast on the diagonal in a criss-cross pattern (do not cut through the breast meat). Season the duck evenly on both sides with the rub. Combine the tea, brown sugar and rice in a small bowl. Pour this mixture down the centre of a 30-by-50 cm/12-by-20-inch sheet of heavy-duty aluminium foil. Fold the long sides over the mixture, and then loosely fold in the shorter ends to create a parcel. Pierce with a skewer to allow smoke to escape.

3 In a small, non-reactive bowl combine the sauce ingredients. Set aside.

4 Brush the cooking grate clean. Preheat a 30-cm/12-inch cast-iron frying pan over GRILLING/DIRECT MEDIUM HEAT for 5 minutes. Lay the duck in the frying pan, skin side down, and sear for 2–3 minutes until the skin is crisp and golden. Remove the duck from the frying pan and set aside. Wearing insulated barbecue gloves, carefully remove the frying pan from the grill.

5 Place the tea parcel, with the seam side up, directly on the charcoal. When the parcel begins to smoke, place the duck breasts, skin side up, over ROASTING/INDIRECT MEDIUM HEAT above the tray of water. Close the lid and smoke the duck breasts until cooked to your desired doneness, about 8 minutes for medium. Remove from the grill and leave to rest for 3–5 minutes. Serve the duck warm with the sauce.

# CHICKEN SOUVLAKI SANDWICHES
## WITH TZATZIKI SAUCE

IDEAL
GRILL:

SMOKE INTENSITY: moderate

PREP TIME: 25 minutes

CHILLING TIME: at least 1 hour

COOKING TIME: 9–13 minutes

SERVES: 6

### TZATZIKI

240 ml/8 fl oz plain Greek yogurt
½ large cucumber, finely chopped
2 tablespoons tahini
2 tablespoons fresh lemon juice
1 tablespoon finely chopped fresh dill
1 garlic clove, finely chopped

Sea salt
Ground black pepper

### RUB

2 teaspoons ground cumin
2 teaspoons ground coriander

4 boneless, skinless chicken breasts,
    each about 175 g/6 oz
2 tablespoons extra-virgin olive oil

1 large handful oak wood chips,
    soaked in water for at least 30
    minutes
6 wholewheat pitta breads, tops
    cut off
½ iceberg lettuce, shredded
3 ripe plum tomatoes, each cut into
    5-mm/¼-inch slices
½ red onion, thinly sliced

1 Combine the tzatziki ingredients in a medium, non-reactive bowl. Season with salt and pepper. Cover and refrigerate for at least 1 hour or up to 1 day.

2 Mix the rub ingredients, including ¾ teaspoon salt and ½ teaspoon pepper, in a small bowl. Brush the chicken breasts on both sides with the oil and season evenly with the rub.

3 Prepare a two-zone fire for medium heat (180–230°C/350–450°F) (see pages 20–22).

4 Brush the cooking grate clean. Drain and add the wood chips to the charcoal and put the lid on the grill. When the wood begins to smoke, cook the chicken, smooth (skin) side down first, over GRILLING/DIRECT MEDIUM HEAT for 8–12 minutes, with the lid closed as much as possible, turning once or twice, until the meat is firm to the touch and opaque all the way to the centre. Remove from the grill and leave to rest for 3–5 minutes. Cut the chicken crossways into ½-inch slices.

5 Grill the pitta breads over GRILLING/DIRECT MEDIUM HEAT for about 1 minute, with the lid closed and turning once, until warmed. Remove from the grill and fill with chicken, tzatziki, lettuce, tomatoes, and onion. Serve warm.

*Leftover tzatziki sauce makes an excellent dip for pitta chips or raw vegetables. The sauce can be refrigerated for up to 3 days.*

# HICKORY-BARBECUED CHICKEN

IDEAL
GRILL:

SMOKE INTENSITY: moderate

PREP TIME: 20 minutes

COOKING TIME: 41–45 minutes

SERVES: 4

## RUB

2 teaspoons paprika

2 teaspoons sea salt

½ teaspoon garlic granules

½ teaspoon ground black pepper

4 whole chicken legs, each 300–375
    g/10–12 oz, cut into thighs and
    drumsticks

## SAUCE

240 ml/8 fl oz tomato ketchup

4 tablespoons cider vinegar

1 tablespoon soft light brown sugar

1 tablespoon Dijon mustard

2 teaspoons hot pepper sauce

2 large handfuls hickory wood chips,
    soaked in water for at least
    30 minutes

*Grill the chicken with the skin side down first to melt the fat under the skin. This will help the skin develop a somewhat crispy texture, even when you brush the sauce all over it.*

1 Mix the rub ingredients in a small bowl. Season the chicken thighs and drumsticks all over with the rub.

2 Prepare the grill for direct and roasting/indirect cooking over medium heat (180–230°C/350–450°F) (see pages 26–27).

3 Combine the sauce ingredients in a medium saucepan. Bring to a simmer over a medium heat and cook for 6–8 minutes, stirring occasionally, until slightly thickened.

4 Brush the cooking grates clean. Cook the chicken, skin side down first, over GRILLING/DIRECT MEDIUM HEAT for 6-10 minutes with the lid closed as much as possible and turning occasionally, until golden brown. Move the chicken over ROASTING/INDIRECT MEDIUM HEAT. Drain and add the wood chips to the smoker box of a gas grill, following manufacturer's instructions. Close the lid and continue cooking for about 35 minutes until the juices run clear and the meat is opaque all the way to the bone, basting with the sauce and turning several times during the last 20 minutes of cooking time. Remove from the grill and leave to rest for 3–5 minutes. Serve warm or at room temperature with any remaining sauce on the side.

# TANDOORI-MARINATED CHICKEN
## WITH INDIAN CORN RELISH

**IDEAL GRILL:**

**SMOKE INTENSITY:** strong

**PREP TIME:** 30 minutes

**MARINATING TIME:** 6–8 hours

**COOKING TIME:** about 1¼ hours

**SPECIAL EQUIPMENT:** large disposable foil tray

**SERVES:** 6

### MARINADE
350 ml/12 fl oz plain Greek yogurt
1 small onion, chopped
2 tablespoons chopped fresh ginger
2 tablespoons fresh lemon juice
2 tablespoons curry powder
2 tablespoons paprika
4 garlic cloves, roughly chopped
¼ teaspoon ground cayenne pepper
Sea salt

6 whole chicken legs, each 300–375
 g/10–12 oz, skin removed

### RELISH
2 fresh corn cobs, outer leaves and
 silk removed
3 plum tomatoes, deseeded, cut into
 1-cm/½-inch dice
1 red onion, finely chopped
2 tablespoons fresh coriander, finely
 chopped
2 teaspoons peeled fresh ginger,
 finely chopped
3 tablespoons cider vinegar
2 teaspoons granulated sugar
½ teaspoon ground cumin
½ teaspoon ground coriander
¼ teaspoon ground cinnamon
¼ teaspoon crushed red chilli flakes

2 large handfuls apple wood chips,
 soaked in water for at least
 30 minutes

1  Combine the marinade ingredients, including 2 teaspoons salt, in a food processor and process until smooth.

2  Put the chicken in a large glass baking dish. Pour the marinade over the chicken and turn to coat. Cover and refrigerate for 6–8 hours, turning once.

3  Prepare a two-zone fire for medium heat (180–230°C/350–450°F) (see pages 20–22).

4  Brush the cooking grate clean. Cook the corn over GRILLING/DIRECT MEDIUM HEAT for 10–12 minutes, with the lid closed as much as possible and turning occasionally, until browned in spots and tender. Remove from the grill and, when cool enough to handle, cut the kernels off the cobs. Mix all of the relish ingredients in a large, non-reactive bowl. Season with ¼ teaspoon salt. Cover and refrigerate for at least 2 hours to blend the flavours.

5  Prepare a two-zone fire for high heat (230–290°C/450–550°F). Place a large disposable foil tray beside the bed of charcoal and fill three-quarters full with water.

6  Remove the chicken from the dish (do not remove the marinade that clings to the chicken). Brush the cooking grate clean. Drain and add one handful of the wood chips to the charcoal and put the lid on the grill. When the wood begins to smoke, cook the chicken, bone side down, over ROASTING/INDIRECT HIGH HEAT for about 1 hour, with the lid closed, until the juices run clear and the meat is no longer pink at the bone. After 30 minutes of cooking time, drain and add the remaining wood chips to the charcoal. Remove the chicken from the grill and leave to rest for 3–5 minutes. Serve warm with the relish.

*The chicken legs that you set closest to the charcoal are bound to cook faster than the others, so swap their positions once or twice for even cooking.*

# POMEGRANATE-GLAZED QUAIL
## WITH DRIED CHERRIES AND WALNUTS

IDEAL GRILL:

SMOKE INTENSITY: moderate

PREP TIME: 20 minutes

MARINATING TIME: 8-24 hours

COOKING TIME: about 16 minutes

SERVES: 4

*Many marinades (like this one) can double as salad dressings. However, note that some of the marinade is set aside for this purpose. Never use marinade that has come into contact with raw meat for a salad dressing.*

### MARINADE
3 tablespoons pomegranate
    black treacle
3 tablespoons balsamic vinegar
2 teaspoons finely chopped
    fresh thyme
¾ teaspoon sea salt
½ teaspoon crushed red chilli flakes
240 ml/8 fl oz extra-virgin olive oil

8 whole quail, backbones and wing
    tips removed, butterflied
Sea salt
Ground black pepper
1 large handful oak wood chips,
    soaked in water for at least
    30 minutes

### SALAD
1 heart of cos lettuce, cut crossways
    into thin strips
75 g/3 oz dried tart cherries, roughly
    chopped
50 g/2 oz walnuts, coarsely chopped

1 Whisk the black treacle, vinegar, thyme, salt and red chilli flakes in a small bowl. Gradually whisk in the oil. Pour 120 ml/4 fl oz of the marinade into a small, non-reactive bowl to use for the salad. Cover and refrigerate until ready to use. Place the quail in a large resealable plastic bag and pour in the remaining marinade. Press the air out of the bag and seal tightly. Turn the bag to distribute the marinade, place in a bowl and refrigerate for at least 8 hours or up to 24 hours, turning occasionally.

2 Prepare a two-zone fire for high heat (230–290°C/450–550°F) (see pages 20–22).

3 Remove the quail from the bag, letting the excess marinade drip back into the bag. Discard the marinade. Season the quail with 1 teaspoon salt and ½ teaspoon pepper. Brush the cooking grate clean. Drain and add the wood chips to the charcoal and put the lid on the grill. When smoke appears, cook the quail, breast side up, over ROASTING/INDIRECT HIGH HEAT for about 15 minutes, with the lid closed, until the meat shows no sign of pink when pierced with the tip of a knife at the thigh bone. To crisp the skin, move the quail over GRILLING/DIRECT HIGH HEAT, skin side down, and cook for about 1 minute, turning once. Remove from the grill.

4 In a large bowl toss the salad ingredients with the reserved, refrigerated marinade. Season with salt and pepper. Serve the quail warm with the salad.

# BUTTERFLIED CURRY CHICKEN

IDEAL
GRILL:

SMOKE INTENSITY: moderate

PREP TIME: 15 minutes

COOKING TIME: 1¾–2¼ hours

SPECIAL EQUIPMENT: poultry
shears, instant-read meat
thermometer

SERVES: 4

*Whole chicken has such an
irregular shape that it is
challenging to cook it evenly.
Butterflying the chicken helps
a lot, as it creates a relatively
even shape. Cooking the chicken
slowly also helps.*

## RUB

1 tablespoon granulated sugar

1 tablespoon sea salt

1 tablespoon curry powder

½ teaspoon garlic granules

¼ teaspoon ground cayenne pepper

1 chicken, about 2.5 kg/5 lb, giblets
    and any excess fat removed

4 large handfuls apple wood chips,
    soaked in water for at least
    30 minutes

50 g/2 oz unsalted butter, melted

1 Combine the rub ingredients in a small bowl. Place the chicken, breast side down, on a chopping board. Using poultry shears, cut from the neck to the tail end, along either side of the backbone. Remove the backbone. Once the backbone is out, you'll be able to see the interior of the chicken. Make a small slit in the cartilage at the bottom end of the breastbone. Then, placing both hands on the rib cage, crack the chicken open like a book. Run your fingers along either side of the cartilage in between the breast to loosen it from the flesh. Grab the bone and pull up on it to remove it along with the attached cartilage. The chicken should now lie flat. Season the chicken evenly on all sides with the rub.

2 Prepare the grill for roasting/indirect cooking over low heat (130–180°C/250–350°F) (see pages 26–27).

3 Brush the cooking grates clean. When the temperature of the grill reaches 170°C/325°F, drain and add two handfuls of the wood chips to the smoker box of a gas grill, following manufacturer's instructions, and close the lid. When the wood begins to smoke, cook the chicken, bone side down, over ROASTING/INDIRECT LOW HEAT for 1¾–2¼ hours, with the lid closed, until the juices run clear and an instant-read meat thermometer inserted into the thickest part of the thigh (not touching the bone) reaches 70–74°C/160–165°F. Lightly brush the chicken with melted butter every 30 minutes, and drain and add the remaining wood chips to the smoker box after the first 30 minutes. When the chicken is done, remove it from the grill and leave to rest for 5 to 10 minutes (the internal temperature will rise 5–10 degrees during this time).

4 Cut the chicken into serving pieces. Serve warm.

# MESQUITE BEER CAN CHICKEN

IDEAL GRILL:

SMOKE INTENSITY: moderate

PREP TIME: 15 minutes

COOKING TIME: 1¼–1½ hours

SPECIAL EQUIPMENT: large disposable foil tray, instant-read meat thermometer

SERVES: 4

## RUB
1 teaspoon garlic granules
1 teaspoon prepared chilli seasoning
1 teaspoon sea salt
½ teaspoon ground black pepper

1 chicken, 2–2.5 kg/4–5 lb, giblets and any excess fat removed
Extra-virgin olive oil

1 can (350 ml/12 fl oz) beer, at room temperature
4 large handfuls mesquite wood chips, soaked in water for at least 30 minutes

*If standing a whole chicken on a beer can sounds wacky to you, put aside your scepticism for a moment and think about how tender and juicy the chicken will be when it is cooked from the inside with steaming beer. Then imagine what the aromatic wood smoke will do to flavour the spice-rubbed skin. Now you have some idea of why this technique has achieved legendary status in the world of American barbecue. The trickiest part of the process may be getting the hot can out of the chicken. To do so, get a good grip on the neck and back of the chicken with tongs, lift the chicken up, and then, using another pair of tongs, pull out the can.*

1 Prepare a two-zone fire for medium heat (180–230°C/350–450°F) (see pages 20–22). Place a large disposable foil tray beside the bed of charcoal and fill three-quarters full with water.

2 Mix the rub ingredients in a small bowl. Lightly coat the chicken all over with oil and season evenly with the rub. Fold the wing tips behind the chicken's back.

3 Open the can of beer and pour out about half. Using a can opener, make two more holes in the top of the can. Place the can on a solid surface, and then lower the chicken cavity over the can.

4 Brush the cooking grate clean. Drain and add the wood chips to the charcoal and put the lid on the grill. When the wood begins to smoke, transfer the chicken-on-a-can to the grill, balancing it on its two legs and the can, like a tripod. Cook the chicken over ROASTING/INDIRECT MEDIUM HEAT for 1¼–1½ hours, with the lid closed, until the juices run clear and the internal temperature registers 70–74°C/160–165°F in the thickest part of the thigh (not touching the bone). Replenish the charcoal as needed to maintain a steady temperature, adding 6 to 10 lit briquettes after 45 minutes.

5 Carefully remove the chicken-on-a-can from the grill (do not spill the contents of the beer can, as it will be very hot). Leave to rest for 5–10 minutes (the internal temperature will rise 5–10 degrees during this time) before lifting it from the can and cutting it into serving pieces. Serve warm.

# WHOLE ROASTED DUCK

## WITH PINEAPPLE CHUTNEY

IDEAL GRILL:

SMOKE INTENSITY: moderate

PREP TIME: 30 minutes

STEAMING TIME: about 1½ hours

COOLING TIME: 1 hour

REFRIGERATION TIME: 12–24 hours

COOKING TIME: about 1 hour

SPECIAL EQUIPMENT: roasting rack, 3 large disposable foil trays, instant-read meat thermometer

SERVES: 4

1 duck, about 3 kg/6 lb, giblets, neck and wing tips removed
2 teaspoons sea salt
½ teaspoon ground black pepper
2 whole star anise
1 cinnamon stick, about 7 cm/ 3 inches long

### CHUTNEY

500 g/1 lb peeled, cored fresh pineapple, cut into 5-mm/ ¼-inch dice
4 tablespoons soft light brown sugar
½ red onion, finely chopped
3 tablespoons unseasoned rice vinegar
1½ tablespoons peeled fresh ginger, finely chopped
1 whole star anise
1 cinnamon stick, about 7 cm/ 3 inches long
¼ teaspoon deseeded bird's eye or serrano chilli, finely chopped

4 large handfuls cherry wood chips, soaked in water for at least 30 minutes

*Steaming the duck helps melt some of the excess fat from its skin. Refrigerating the duck overnight dries and tightens the skin to help it release even more fat during cooking.*

1 Using a meat fork, pierce the duck skin all over, especially the breast and thigh areas, taking care not to pierce the flesh. Season the duck inside and outside with the salt and pepper. Put the star anise and the cinnamon stick inside the body cavity.

2 Preheat the oven to 180°C/350°F/Gas mark 4. Place the duck on a roasting rack and set it inside a large disposable foil tray. Add 1 litre/1¾ pints of warm water to the tray. Invert another foil tray and use it to cover the duck. Steam the duck for about 1½ hours, covered, in the oven, until the skin shrinks around the legs and thighs and most of the fat has rendered out. Remove from the oven and leave to cool at room temperature for 1 hour. Refrigerate the cooled duck, uncovered, for 12–24 hours.

3 Bring the chutney ingredients to a simmer in a medium saucepan over a medium heat. Cook for about 20 minutes, stirring often, until the pineapple is translucent and the chutney has reduced to about 240 ml/8 fl oz. Transfer to a non-reactive bowl and remove the star anise and the cinnamon stick. Leave to cool.

4 Prepare a two-zone fire for medium heat (180–230°C/350–450°F) (see pages 20–22). Place a large disposable foil tray beside the bed of charcoal and fill three-quarters full with water.

5 Brush the cooking grate clean. Drain and add two handfuls of the wood chips to the charcoal and put the lid on the grill. When the wood begins to smoke, cook the duck over ROASTING/INDIRECT MEDIUM HEAT for 30 minutes, with the lid closed. Drain and add the remaining wood chips to the charcoal. Continue cooking for about 30 minutes more, with the lid closed, until an instant-read meat thermometer inserted into the thickest part of the thigh (not touching the bone) registers 77°C/170°F. If liked, move the duck over GRILLING/DIRECT MEDIUM HEAT to crisp the skin for a few minutes, turning occasionally, but be careful that the skin does not burn. Remove from the grill and leave to rest for about 15 minutes (the internal temperature will rise 5–10 degrees during this time).

6 Cut the duck into serving pieces and serve hot with the chutney.

# BARBECUED TURKEY DRUMSTICKS
## WITH CHILLI DRY RUB

IDEAL
GRILL:

SMOKE INTENSITY: **strong**

PREP TIME: **15 minutes**

BRINING TIME: **2 hours**

COOKING TIME: **about 3 hours**

SPECIAL EQUIPMENT: **instant-read meat thermometer**

SERVES: **8**

### BRINE

3 bottles (each 350 ml/12 fl oz) lager
900 ml/1½ pints water
75 g/3 oz sea salt
125 g/4 oz soft light brown sugar

8 turkey drumsticks or thighs, each
     about 375 g/12 oz

### RUB

4 tablespoons chilli powder
2 teaspoons dried oregano
1 teaspoon garlic granules
1 teaspoon ground cumin

6 small mesquite wood chunks

*Turkey drumsticks and thighs,
both dark meat cuts, work
equally well with this recipe.
Turkey thighs are often more
difficult to obtain, but the meat
is easy to cut off the bone in
large chunks.*

1 Stir the brine ingredients in a wide, non-reactive pot until the salt and sugar are dissolved. Put the turkey drumsticks in the brine and then place a plate on top to keep them submerged. Cover and refrigerate for 2 hours.

2 Mix the rub ingredients in a small bowl.

3 Prepare the smoker for roasting/indirect cooking with very low heat (95–130°C/ 200–250°F) (see pages 23–25). When the temperature reaches 110°C/225°F, add two of the wood chunks to the charcoal.

4 Remove the drumsticks from the container and discard the brine. Rinse them under cold running water and pat dry with kitchen paper. Coat the drumsticks with the rub.

5 Brush the cooking grate clean. Smoke the drumsticks over ROASTING/INDIRECT VERY LOW HEAT for about 3 hours, with the lid closed, until the skin is dark brown, the meat is tender at the bone and an instant-read meat thermometer inserted into the thickest part of the drumstick (not touching the bone) registers 82°C/180°F. After the first and second hours, add two more wood chunks and more lit briquettes as necessary to maintain the heat.

6 Remove the drumsticks from the smoker and leave to rest for 5–10 minutes. Serve warm.

# SMOKED TURKEY BREAST
## WITH HONEY MUSTARD

IDEAL GRILL:

SMOKE INTENSITY: **strong**

PREP TIME: **15 minutes**

BRINING TIME: **5 hours**

REFRIGERATION TIME: **12–16 hours**

COOKING TIME: **about 4 hours**

SPECIAL EQUIPMENT: **instant-read meat thermometer**

SERVES: **8**

### BRINE
2 litres/3½ pints water
75 g/3 oz sea salt
175 g/6 oz runny honey
2 teaspoons dried rosemary
2 teaspoons dried sage
1½ teaspoons dried marjoram
1 teaspoon black peppercorns
2 bay leaves

1 whole turkey breast (with bone and
    skin), about 2.75 kg/5½ lb

### MUSTARD
120 ml/4 fl oz Dijon mustard
3 tablespoons runny honey
2 tablespoons soft light brown sugar

8 small apple wood chunks

*Be sure to use a fresh turkey breast for brining. Most frozen turkey breasts are injected with a sodium solution to replace the juices lost during the freezing process. If you brine a turkey breast that has already been treated with salt, you are essentially brining a product that has already been salted. The result could be way too salty.*

1 Whisk the brine ingredients in a large, non-reactive pot until the salt is dissolved. Put the turkey breast in the brine. Put a plate on top of the turkey breast to keep it submerged, cover and refrigerate for 5 hours.

2 Remove the turkey breast from the container and discard the brine. Rinse under cold running water and pat dry with kitchen paper. Place on a wire rack set over a rimmed roasting tray. Refrigerate, uncovered, for 12 to 16 hours to dry the skin.

3 Prepare the smoker for roasting/indirect cooking with very low heat (95–130°C/200–250°F) (see pages 23–25). When the temperature reaches 110°C/225°F, add two wood chunks to the charcoal.

4 Mix the mustard ingredients in a small bowl until the brown sugar is dissolved. Cover and set aside at room temperature until ready to serve.

5 Brush the cooking grate clean. Smoke the turkey over ROASTING/INDIRECT VERY LOW HEAT for about 4 hours, with the lid closed, until the skin is dark brown, the meat is tender at the bone, and an instant-read meat thermometer inserted into the thickest part of the breast (not touching the bone) reaches 70–74°C/160–165°F. After the first, second and third hours, add two more wood chunks and more lit briquettes as necessary to maintain the heat. Remove from the smoker and let rest for 5–10 minutes (the internal temperature will rise 5–10 degrees during this time).

6 Carve the turkey breast into thin slices. Serve warm with the honey mustard on the side.

# APPLE-SMOKED TURKEY
## WITH CALVADOS GRAVY

**IDEAL GRILL:**

**SMOKE INTENSITY:** moderate

**PREP TIME:** 45 minutes

**COOKING TIME:** 3–3½ hours

**SPECIAL EQUIPMENT:** 2 large disposable foil trays, roasting rack, instant-read meat thermometer, gravy separator

**SERVES:** 8–12

### BUTTER
75 g/3 oz unsalted butter, softened
2 teaspoons dried rosemary
2 teaspoons dried sage
2 teaspoons dried thyme
½ teaspoon garlic granules
½ teaspoon onion granules

1 turkey, about 6.5 kg/13 lb, thawed
    if necessary
Sea salt
Ground black pepper
1 small onion, peeled and quartered
1 tart apple, such as Granny Smith,
    cored and quartered
750 ml/1¼ pints chicken stock *or*
    turkey stock

6 large handfuls apple wood chips,
    soaked in water for at least
    30 minutes

### GRAVY
240–475 ml/8–16 fl oz chicken stock
    *or* turkey stock, if needed
40 g/1½ oz unsalted butter, melted,
    if needed
50 g/2 oz all-purpose flour
4 tablespoons calvados

*Do not use a high-quality metal roasting tin, as the smoke may discolour it.*

1  Mix the butter ingredients in a small bowl.

2  Remove the giblets and neck from the turkey and reserve for another use. Rinse the turkey, inside and outside, under cold water and pat dry with kitchen paper. Tuck the wing tips behind the turkey's back. Generously rub the turkey with the herb butter and then season evenly, inside and outside, with 1 tablespoon salt and 1 teaspoon pepper. Stuff the turkey with the onion and apple. Cover the entire turkey breast with aluminium foil, but don't cover the wings or thighs.

3  Place one large disposable foil tray inside the other. Pour 750 ml/1¼ pints stock into the top tray. Place the turkey on a roasting rack, breast side down, and set it inside the trays. Leave the turkey to stand at room temperature for 1 hour before cooking.

4  Prepare the grill for roasting/indirect cooking over low heat (130–180°C/ 250–350°F).

5  Brush the cooking grates clean. Drain and add two handfuls of wood chips to the smoker box of a gas grill, following manufacturer's instructions, and close the lid. When the wood begins to smoke, cook the turkey in the trays over ROASTING/ INDIRECT LOW HEAT for 45 minutes, with the lid closed. Drain and add another two handfuls of wood chips to the smoker box, and continue cooking the turkey for 45 minutes more.

6  After 1½ hours, wearing insulated barbecue gloves and using a pair of tongs, turn the turkey over so that the breast side is facing up. Remove and discard the foil. Drain and add the remaining two handfuls of wood chips to the smoker box. Continue cooking the turkey for 1½–2 hours more until it is golden brown and an instant-read meat thermometer inserted in the thickest part of the thigh (not touching the bone) reaches 77–80°C/170–175°F.

7  Carefully remove the turkey and the trays from the grill. Tilt the turkey so the juices run out of the body cavity and into the trays. Transfer the turkey to a chopping board and leave to rest for 20–30 minutes (the internal temperature will rise 5–10 degrees during this time). Save the pan juices to make the gravy.

8  Strain the pan juices into a gravy separator. Leave to stand for about 3 minutes until the fat rises to the surface. Pour the juices into a 1-litre/1¾-pints measuring jug, reserving the fat. Add more stock as needed to make 1 litre/1¾ pints.

9  Measure the fat. You should have 120 ml/4 fl oz. Add melted butter if needed. Heat the fat (and butter) in a medium saucepan over medium heat. Whisk in the flour and let bubble for 1 minute, stirring constantly. Whisk in the pan juices and the calvados. Bring to a simmer, whisking often. Reduce the heat to medium-low and simmer for 5–10 minutes until lightly thickened. Remove from the heat and season with salt and pepper.

10  Carve the turkey and serve warm with the gravy.

# Seafood

# NEW ENGLAND CLAMBAKE

**IDEAL GRILL:**

**SMOKE INTENSITY:** moderate

**PREP TIME:** 30 minutes

**COOKING TIME:** about 45 minutes

**SPECIAL EQUIPMENT:** large disposable foil tray

**SERVES:** 4

750 g/1½ lb baby new potatoes

1 tablespoon plus 2 teaspoons extra-virgin olive oil

4 fresh corn cobs, outer leaves and silk removed

250 g/8 oz unsalted butter, cut into pieces

4 dozen small clams, rinsed and scrubbed

180 ml/6 fl oz lager

4 lobster tails, each about 125 g/4 oz, cut in half lengthways

500g/1 lb kingsize prawns (16/20 count), deveined, shells and tails left on

1 large handful pecan wood chips, soaked in water for at least 30 minutes

Sea salt

Ground black pepper

2 lemons, each cut into quarters

*To prepare the lobster tails, use kitchen scissors to cut through the centre of the shell on the underside of each tail. Turn each tail over and cut through the harder back shell all the way to the fins. Cut each tail in half lengthways, passing through the openings you have already made.*

1 Prepare a two-zone fire for high heat (230–290°C/450–550°F) (see pages 20–22). Preheat the oven to 110°C/200°F/Gas mark ¼.

2 Toss the potatoes with 1 tablespoon of the oil in a large bowl. Wrap the potatoes in heavy-duty aluminium foil and create a parcel, crimping the edges tightly. Wrap each corn cob in foil.

3 Cook the parcel of potatoes over **GRILLING/DIRECT HIGH HEAT** for 20 minutes, with the lid closed as much as possible. Carefully turn the parcel over, being careful not to puncture the foil, and then place the corn on the cooking grate. Continue to cook over **GRILLING/DIRECT HIGH HEAT** for about 15 minutes, with the lid closed as much as possible, turning the corn three or four times, until the potatoes and corn are tender. Transfer the potato parcel and corn to a large roasting tray and place in the oven to keep warm.

4 Arrange the coals in a bull's-eye configuration (see photo below), adding enough charcoal briquettes to raise the temperature of the grill back up to high heat. Let the charcoal burn for about 15 minutes until covered with white ash.

5 Meanwhile, cook the butter in a small, heavy saucepan over a medium heat, until melted and boiling. Pour the melted butter into a glass measuring jug and leave to stand for 5 minutes. Skim the foam from the surface. Pour the butter into four individual ramekins, leaving the milky residue at the bottom of the jug. Transfer the ramekins to the roasting tray in the oven to keep warm.

6 Put the clams in a large disposable foil tray and pour in the lager. Cover tightly with aluminium foil. Brush the lobster flesh and the prawns with the remaining 2 teaspoons oil.

7 Brush the cooking grates clean. Drain and add the wood chips to the charcoal and put the lid on the grill. When the wood begins to smoke, place the foil tray with the clams over **GRILLING/DIRECT HIGH HEAT**. Place the lobster, meat side down, and the prawns over **ROASTING/INDIRECT HIGH HEAT**. Close the lid and cook until the clams have opened, the lobster meat is white and firm but not dry, and the prawns are firm to the touch and just turning opaque in the centre, shaking the foil tray after 5 minutes to redistribute the clams and turning the lobster and the prawns once or twice. The clams and lobster will take about 10 minutes and the prawns will take 3–5 minutes. Remove from the grill as they are done.

8 Place the potatoes, corn and clams in separate serving bowls and the lobster and prawns on a serving plate. Season the potatoes and corn with salt and pepper as liked. Serve at once with the melted butter and lemon quarters.

# SMOKY PRAWN TACOS
## WITH CHIPOTLE CREMA

IDEAL GRILL:

**SMOKE INTENSITY:** moderate

**PREP TIME:** 20 minutes

**COOKING TIME:** 5–7 minutes

**SPECIAL EQUIPMENT:** perforated grill pan

**SERVES:** 4

### CREMA
1 mild chilli, deseeded and finely
    chopped
1½ teaspoons chipotle sauce
½ teaspoon finely chopped garlic
120 ml/4 fl oz sour cream

1 small head cos lettuce, cored and
    shredded
2 ripe tomatoes, deseeded and
    chopped
⅓ cucumber, chopped
40 g/1½ oz fresh coriander

1 tablespoon extra-virgin olive oil
½ teaspoon sea salt
¼ teaspoon ground black pepper
500g/1 lb prawns, peeled and
    deveined, tails removed

1 large handful mesquite wood chips,
    soaked in water for at least 30
    minutes

12 corn or flour tortillas (15cm/
    6 inches)
2 limes, cut into wedges
Pickled jalapeño rings (optional)

1 Prepare a two-zone fire for medium heat (180–230°C/350–450°F) (see pages 20–22) and preheat the grill pan on the cooking grate.

2 Using the back of a spoon, mash the chilli, chipotle sauce and garlic into a paste in a small bowl. Stir in the soured cream.

3 Combine the lettuce, tomatoes, cucumber and coriander in a large bowl. Cover and refrigerate until ready to use.

4 Whisk the oil, salt and pepper in a medium bowl. Add the prawns and toss to coat.

5 Brush the cooking grate clean. Drain and add the wood chips to the charcoal and put the lid on the grill. When the wood begins to smoke, spread the prawns in a single layer on the grill pan and cook over **GRILLING/DIRECT MEDIUM HEAT** for 4–6 minutes, with the lid closed as much as possible and turning once, until firm to the touch and just turning opaque in the centre. Transfer to a serving plate. Warm the tortillas over **GRILLING/DIRECT MEDIUM HEAT** for about 15 seconds on each side. Fill each tortilla with some of the lettuce mixture, a few prawns and a drizzle of the crema. Serve immediately, with lime wedges and pickled jalapeño rings, if liked.

*In some cases tortillas soften quickly when moistened by the prawns and crema. If that happens, stack two tortillas together to make a double-thick wrap for the filling.*

# PRAWN AND RICE SAUSAGES
## WITH VIETNAMESE DIPPING SAUCE

**IDEAL GRILL:**

**SMOKE INTENSITY:** moderate

**PREP TIME:** 1 hour

**COOKING TIME:** 6–8 minutes

**SPECIAL EQUIPMENT:** perforated grill pan

**SERVES:** 4–6; 8–12 as a starter

Rapeseed oil
1 tablespoon fish sauce
2 teaspoons granulated sugar
2 spring onions, finely chopped
    (white and light green parts only)
1½ teaspoons baking powder
½ teaspoon ground black pepper
1 kg/2 lb prawns, peeled and
    deveined, tails removed
125 g/4 oz cooked short-grain rice,
    at room temperature

### SAUCE

4 tablespoons fish sauce
4 tablespoons fresh lime juice
4 tablespoons granulated sugar
2 teaspoons deseeded, finely
    chopped bird's eye chilli
½ teaspoon finely chopped garlic

2 large handfuls apple wood chips,
    soaked in water for at least
    30 minutes

2 heads round lettuce, separated into
    leaves
Fresh mint
2 large carrots, peeled and grated
1 cucumber, cut in half lengthways,
    thinly sliced into half-moons

*You can use a food processor, but chopping the prawns with a knife gives a better texture.*

1 Whisk 1 tablespoon oil, the fish sauce and sugar in a large bowl until the sugar dissolves. Stir in the spring onions, baking powder and pepper (the mixture will foam slightly). Chop the prawns into a chunky paste. Add the prawns and rice to the spring onion mixture and mix thoroughly. Working with 2 tablespoons at a time, shape the mixture into 24–30 5-cm/2-inch-long sausages and place on an oiled roasting tray. Brush the top of each sausage with oil.

2 Whisk the sauce ingredients in a small, non-reactive bowl until the sugar is dissolved.

3 Prepare a two-zone fire for low heat (130–180°C/250–350°F) (see pages 20–22) and preheat the grill pan on the cooking grate over grilling/direct heat.

4 Brush the cooking grate clean. Drain and add the wood chips to the charcoal and put the lid on the grill. When the wood begins to smoke, close the bottom vent on the grill and leave the top vent half open. Place the sausages in a single layer on the grill pan and cook over **GRILLING/DIRECT LOW HEAT** for 6–8 minutes with the lid closed as much as possible and turning once, until the sausages are plump, opaque and golden. Remove from the grill.

5 Place each sausage on a lettuce leaf and top with mint, carrots and cucumber. Drizzle with the sauce or use sauce for dipping. Serve warm or at room temperature.

# WARM SALAD OF SMOKED MACKEREL
## AND ORANGE SUPREMES

**IDEAL GRILL:**

**SMOKE INTENSITY:** moderate

**PREP TIME:** 45 minutes

**COOKING TIME:** 10–12 minutes

**SERVES:** 4

*Cook the mackerel at the lower end of the medium heat range, around 180°C/350°F, to allow extra time for the smoke to penetrate the flesh.*

3 large oranges

6 Mackerel fillets, each 12g–150 g/
    4–5 oz
Sea salt
Ground black pepper
2 large handfuls hickory wood chips,
    soaked in water for at least 30
    minutes

1 tablespoon cider vinegar
1 teaspoon Dijon mustard
1 teaspoon runny honey
3 tablespoons extra-virgin olive oil
175 g/6 oz mixed baby salad leaves
12 small pickled onions (from a jar)

1  Prepare a two-zone fire for medium heat (180–230°C/350–450°F) (see pages 20–22).

2  Supreme the oranges: cut off a small slice from the top and bottom of each orange so the round fruit can stand upright. Use a serrated knife to cut the peel off the flesh in long arcs, starting at the top and following down along the natural curve of the fruit. Cut far enough into the flesh to remove the white pith but not so far as to damage the pulp. Then hold the peeled fruit in your hand and use a paring knife to cut between the flesh and the white membranes separating the individual segments. Allow the segments to fall into a bowl.

3  Season the mackerel fillets evenly with ¼ teaspoon salt and ¼ teaspoon pepper. Brush the cooking grate clean. Drain and add the wood chips to the charcoal and put the lid on the grill. When the wood begins to smoke, cook the fillets, skin side down, over **ROASTING/INDIRECT MEDIUM HEAT** for 10–12 minutes, with the lid closed as much as possible (do not turn), until the mackerel just barely begins to flake when you poke it with the tip of a knife. Transfer to a chopping board, leave to cool for a few minutes, and then peel off the skin. Chop the mackerel into bite-sized chunks.

4  Whisk the vinegar, mustard, honey, ¼ teaspoon salt and ¼ teaspoon pepper in a large bowl. Gradually whisk in the oil until the dressing is emulsified. Add the salad leaves and toss to coat. Divide evenly between four serving plates. Top each plate with equal amounts of the orange supremes, mackerel and onions.

# SMOKED FISH FILLETS
## WITH PECAN BROWN BUTTER

IDEAL GRILL:

**SMOKE INTENSITY:** moderate

**PREP TIME:** 20 minutes

**COOKING TIME:** about 12 minutes

**SERVES:** 6

### PASTE
2 garlic cloves
½ teaspoon sea salt
2 tablespoons extra-virgin olive oil
1 tablespoon paprika
2 teaspoons finely chopped thyme
1 teaspoon celery seeds
½ teaspoon ground white pepper
⅛ teaspoon ground cayenne pepper

6  white fish fillets such as sea bass or
    plaice, each about 200 g/7 oz and
    1 cm/½ inch thick

### BUTTER
75 g/3 oz unsalted butter
50 g/2oz pecans, coarsely chopped
1 tablespoon fresh lemon juice
1 tablespoon chopped flat-leaf
    parsley
¼ teaspoon sea salt
⅛ teaspoon ground black pepper

1 large handful pecan wood chips,
    soaked in water for at least
    30 minutes

*If your fish fillets are larger than 200 g/7 oz, just add a few more minutes of cooking time and cook until the fish is opaque when flaked with the tip of a knife.*

1 Finely chop the garlic and then sprinkle with the salt. Use the side of a knife to smash the garlic into a paste. Keep swishing the knife back and forth until the garlic is so thin it's almost transparent. Transfer to a small bowl. Add the remaining paste ingredients and mix to combine thoroughly. Spread the paste on both sides of the fish fillets. Leave the fish to stand at room temperature for about 20 minutes while you preheat the grill.

2 Prepare a two-zone fire for medium heat (180–230°C/350–450°F) (see pages 20–22).

3 Melt the butter in a medium frying pan over a medium heat and cook for about 3 minutes just until it turns light brown. Remove from the heat. Stir in the remaining butter ingredients.

4 Brush the cooking grate clean. Drain and add the wood chips to the charcoal and put the lid on the grill. When the wood begins to smoke, cook the fish over **GRILLING/DIRECT MEDIUM HEAT** for about 12 minutes, with the lid closed as much as possible and carefully turning once, until the fish just barely begins to flake when you poke it with the tip of a knife. Remove from the grill. Serve warm with the butter spooned over the top.

# PROVENÇAL SALMON FILLETS
## WITH SMOKED TOMATOES AND FENNEL

IDEAL
GRILL:

SMOKE INTENSITY: mild

PREP TIME: 20 minutes

COOKING TIME: 22–28 minutes

SPECIAL EQUIPMENT: 8 metal
or bamboo skewers (if using
bamboo, soak in water for at
least 30 minutes); spice mill

SERVES: 4

1 large fennel bulb, about 500 g/
    1 lb, root end and stalks removed
375 g/12 oz cherry tomatoes
Extra-virgin olive oil
Sea salt
Ground black pepper

2 large handfuls hickory wood chips,
    soaked in water for at least
    30 minutes

RUB
2 teaspoons fennel seeds
1 teaspoon herbes de Provence
¼ teaspoon ground cayenne pepper

4 salmon fillets (with skin), each 175–
    250 g/6–8 oz and about 2.5 cm/
    1 inch thick, pin bones removed

*Fennel bulbs separate nicely into layers (similar to onions) and so are perfect for skewering and then smoking over a smouldering fire.*

1 Prepare the grill for grilling/direct cooking over medium heat (180–230°C/350–450°F) (see pages 26–27).

2 Cut the fennel bulb in half lengthways and remove the thick, triangular core. Cut the halves into chunks about three layers thick and about as big as the tomatoes. Thread the fennel and tomatoes on separate skewers, brush them with oil and season with salt and pepper.

3 Brush the cooking grates clean. Drain and add one handful of the wood chips to the smoker box of a gas grill, following manufacturer's instructions, and close the lid. When smoke appears, cook the fennel skewers over **GRILLING/DIRECT MEDIUM HEAT** for 6–8 minutes, with the lid closed. Add the tomato skewers and continue cooking with the fennel over **GRILLING/DIRECT MEDIUM HEAT** for 8–9 minutes more, with the lid closed as much as possible and turning once or twice, until the vegetables are tender and the fennel is lightly browned. Remove from the grill as they are done. Increase the temperature of the grill to high heat (230–290°C/450–550°F).

4 Crush the fennel seed in a spice grinder or pestle and mortar. Pour into a small bowl and mix with the remaining rub ingredients, including 1 teaspoon salt and ½ teaspoon black pepper. Lightly brush the salmon fillets with oil and season evenly with the rub.

5 Brush the cooking grates clean. Drain and add the remaining wood chips to the smoker box and close the lid. When smoke appears, grill the salmon, flesh side down first, over **GRILLING/DIRECT HIGH HEAT** for 6–8 minutes, with the lid closed, until you can lift the fillets off the cooking grate with tongs without sticking. Turn the fillets over and continue cooking to your desired doneness, 2–3 minutes for medium rare. Remove from the grill and serve warm with the fennel and tomato skewers.

# CEDAR-PLANKED SALMON
## WITH APPLE-TARRAGON SALAD

**IDEAL GRILL:**

**SMOKE INTENSITY:** moderate

**PREP TIME:** 30 minutes

**COOKING TIME:** 15–20 minutes

**SPECIAL EQUIPMENT:** 1 untreated cedar plank, 30–37 cm/ 12–15 inches long and about 18 cm/7 inches wide and 1–1.5 cm/½–¾ inch thick, soaked in water for at least 1 hour

**SERVES:** 4

### SALAD

2 tablespoons soured cream

2 tablespoons fresh lemon juice

¼ teaspoon granulated sugar

2 Granny Smith apples, cut into 5-mm/¼-inch pieces

1 tablespoon finely chopped fresh tarragon

Sea salt

Ground black pepper

### GLAZE

150 ml/¼ pint unsweetened apple juice

1 tablespoon wholegrain mustard

### RUB

1 teaspoon sea salt

½ teaspoon ground black pepper

½ teaspoon granulated sugar

1 salmon fillet (with skin), about 750 g/1½ lb, pin bones removed

2 tablespoons finely chopped fresh tarragon

1 tablespoon finely chopped spring onion (white and light green parts only)

1 Whisk the sour cream, lemon juice and sugar in a medium, non-reactive bowl. Add the apples and tarragon and toss to coat. Season with salt and pepper. Cover and refrigerate until ready to serve.

2 Boil the apple juice in a small saucepan over a high heat for 12–15 minutes, until it is reduced to 3 tablespoons. Remove from the heat and stir in the mustard. Pour the glaze into a small bowl and leave to cool.

3 Prepare a two-zone fire for medium heat (180–230°C/350–450°F) (see pages 20–22).

4 Combine the rub ingredients in a small bowl. Cut the salmon fillet in half lengthways and then crossways to make four individual portions, cutting right down to the skin but not through it. Season the flesh side of the fish evenly with the tarragon and spring onion and then the rub.

5 Brush the cooking grate clean. Place the soaked plank on the cooking grate over **GRILLING/DIRECT MEDIUM HEAT** and close the lid. After 5–10 minutes, when the plank begins to smoke and char, place the fish on the plank and cook over **GRILLING/DIRECT MEDIUM HEAT**, with the lid closed, brushing with the glaze after the first 10 minutes of cooking time, until lightly browned on the surface and cooked to your desired doneness, 15–20 minutes for medium rare. (The cooking time will vary according to the thickness of the fish.) Using sturdy tongs, carefully transfer the fish on the plank to a heatproof surface.

6 Slide a spatula between the skin and flesh and transfer the portions of salmon to individual plates. Serve warm or at room temperature with the salad.

*If at any point you see a lot of smoke pouring out of the grill, move the plank temporarily over roasting/indirect heat.*

# JUNIPER-LACED HOT-SMOKED SALMON

**IDEAL GRILL:**

**SMOKE INTENSITY:** strong

**PREP TIME:** 15 minutes

**REFRIGERATION TIME:** 4½ hours

**STANDING TIME:** 30 minutes, or for delayed smoking, 8–12 hours

**COOKING TIME:** about 2½ hours

**SPECIAL EQUIPMENT:** pestle and mortar, electric fan

**SERVES:** 8

*Some fish fillets look completely boneless, but if you run a fingertip over their surface you might feel the ends of tiny bones, called pin bones, which must be removed. Use a pin-boner or tweezers to grab the end of each bone and carefully pull it out at an angle.*

120 ml/4 fl oz gin
1 salmon fillet (with skin), about
     1.5 kg/3 lb, pin bones removed
4 tablespoons juniper berries
2 teaspoons black peppercorns
250 g/8 oz soft light brown sugar
75 g/3 oz sea salt
1 tablespoon vegetable oil

3 fist-sized pecan wood chunks

1 Pour the gin into a 37-by-25-cm/15-by-10-inch glass or china baking dish. Place the salmon in the dish, skin side up, and spoon the gin all over the fish. Cover and refrigerate for 30 minutes.

2 Using a pestle and mortar coarsely grind 2 tablespoons of the juniper berries and the peppercorns (or crush under a heavy saucepan on a chopping board). Pour the mixture into a medium bowl and combine with the brown sugar and salt. Remove the salmon from the dish and pat dry with kitchen paper. Discard the gin. Wash and dry the dish. Put about one-third of the brown sugar mixture in the dish. Place the salmon, skin side down, in the dish. Spread and pat the remaining brown sugar mixture over the flesh, covering it entirely. Cover and refrigerate for 4 hours.

3 Prepare the smoker for roasting/indirect cooking with very low heat (95–130°C/ 200–250°F) (see pages 23–25).

4 Soak the remaining 2 tablespoons juniper berries in water in a small bowl while cooking the salmon.

5 Remove the salmon from the dish. Rinse under cold running water to remove the brown sugar mixture. Pat dry with kitchen paper. Brush the salmon skin with the oil. Place the salmon on a large wire rack set over a large, rimmed roasting tray. Leave to stand at room temperature for about 30 minutes, with a table fan directed on the salmon until the surface looks lightly glazed and feels tacky. (Or refrigerate the salmon on the rack setup, uncovered, for 8 to 12 hours.)

6 Brush the cooking grate clean. Add one wood chunk to the charcoal. Smoke the salmon fillet, skin side down, over **ROASTING/INDIRECT VERY LOW HEAT** for about 2½ hours, with the lid closed, until the salmon is firm and has a golden, almost deep brown patina. Add more lit briquettes as necessary to maintain the heat. Every 45 minutes, add one more wood chunk to the charcoal. During the last 15 minutes of cooking time, drain and add the juniper berries to the charcoal. Remove the salmon from the smoker and leave to rest for about 5 minutes. Serve warm.

*Once smoked, the salmon can be wrapped in clingfilm and frozen for up to 4 months.*

# DIJON SALMON STRIPS
## ON ORANGE CARPACCIO

IDEAL GRILL:

SMOKE INTENSITY: mild

PREP TIME: 15 minutes

COOKING TIME: 8–12 minutes

SPECIAL EQUIPMENT: large disposable foil roasting tray

SERVES: 4–6

*For the best taste possible, use wild salmon.*

### GLAZE
1 tablespoon wholegrain Dijon mustard
1 tablespoon mayonnaise
2 teaspoons mustard seeds
2 teaspoons soft light brown sugar
⅛ teaspoon ground cayenne pepper

Extra-virgin olive oil
1 large skinless salmon fillet, about 750 g/1½ lb and 1–1.5 cm/¾–1 inch thick, pin bones removed
¼ teaspoon sea salt
⅛ teaspoon ground black pepper

3 large oranges

2 large handfuls apple wood chips, soaked in water for at least 30 minutes
1 tablespoon roughly chopped fresh basil
¼ teaspoon crushed red chilli flakes

1 Mix the glaze ingredients in a small bowl.

2 Lightly coat the bottom of a large disposable foil tray with oil. Cut the salmon across into 8–10 equal pieces and transfer them to the tray, flesh side up. Season the top of the salmon fillets evenly with the salt and pepper and then spread on the glaze. Cover the tray and refrigerate until ready to cook.

3 Prepare the grill for roasting/indirect cooking over medium heat (180–230°C/350–450°F) (see pages 26–27).

4 Cut off a small slice from the top and bottom of each orange so the round fruit can stand upright. Use a serrated knife to cut the peel off the flesh in long arcs, starting at the top and following down along the natural curve of the fruit. Cut far enough into the flesh to remove the white pith but not so far as to damage the pulp. Cut each orange crossways into 2.5-mm/⅛-inch slices. Arrange the orange slices on the bottom of a serving platter. Drizzle about 1 teaspoon oil over the orange slices.

5 Brush the cooking grates clean. Drain and add the wood chips to the smoker box of a gas grill, following manufacturer's instructions, and close the lid. When smoke is pouring out of the grill, set the pan with the salmon over **ROASTING/INDIRECT MEDIUM HEAT**, close the lid (do not turn) and cook to your desired doneness, 8–12 minutes for medium rare. Remove from the grill and arrange the salmon pieces on top of the orange slices. Garnish with the basil and red chilli flakes. Serve warm.

# TERIYAKI TUNA AND PINEAPPLE KEBABS

IDEAL GRILL:

SMOKE INTENSITY: moderate

PREP TIME: 30 minutes

MARINATING TIME: 1 hour

COOKING TIME: 6–8 minutes

SPECIAL EQUIPMENT: 4–6 metal or bamboo skewers (if using bamboo, soak in water for at least 30 minutes)

SERVES: 4–6

## MARINADE

120 ml/4 fl oz pineapple juice, preferably chilled rather than canned

120 ml/4 fl oz soy sauce

50 g/2 oz soft light brown sugar

2 tablespoons thinly sliced dark green spring onion tops

1 tablespoon grated fresh ginger

2 teaspoons finely chopped garlic

1 kg/2 lb tuna steaks, cut into 3.5-cm/1½-inch cubes

2 red peppers, cut into 3.5-cm/1½-inch pieces

6 large spring onions (white and light green parts only), cut into 3.5-cm/1½-inch pieces

250 g/8 oz fresh pineapple, cut into 3.5-cm/1½-inch chunks

Extra-virgin olive oil

2 large handfuls apple wood chips, soaked in water for at least 30 minutes

*When making kebabs, it's important that all pieces of food are about the same size to promote even cooking.*

1  Whisk the marinade ingredients in a large, non-reactive bowl until the sugar dissolves. Add the tuna and gently turn to coat. Cover and refrigerate for 1 hour, turning occasionally.

2  Prepare a two-zone fire for medium heat (180–230°C/350–450°F) (see pages 20–22).

3  Thread the peppers, spring onions, and pineapple alternately on to skewers, leaving a little room between each piece. Thread the tuna on separate skewers. Lightly brush the vegetables and the tuna with oil.

4  Brush the cooking grate clean. Drain and add the wood chips to the charcoal and put the lid on the grill. When the wood begins to smoke, cook the kebabs over **GRILLING/DIRECT MEDIUM HEAT** for 6–8 minutes, with the lid closed as much as possible and turning once or twice, until the vegetables are crisp-tender, the pineapple is lightly browned and the tuna is just pink at the centre. Remove from the grill and serve immediately.

# CEDAR-PLANKED TUNA SALAD
## WITH HONEY-DIJON DRESSING AND CRISPY PECANS

**IDEAL
GRILL:**

**SMOKE INTENSITY:** mild

**PREP TIME:** 15 minutes

**COOKING TIME:** 22-31 minutes

**SPECIAL EQUIPMENT:** perforated grill pan; 1 untreated cedar plank, 30-37 cm/12-15 inches long and about 18 cm/7 inches wide and 1-1.5 cm/½-¾ inch thick, soaked in water for at least 1 hour

**SERVES:** 4-6

*Cedar planks come in different thicknesses. For this recipe, the plank is about 1 cm/½ inch thick, but if you use a thinner one, the cooking time will be shorter.*

### DRESSING
3 tablespoons runny honey
3 tablespoons Dijon mustard
2 tablespoons white wine vinegar
4 tablespoons extra-virgin olive oil
Sea salt

50 g/2 oz pecan halves
250 g/8 oz sugar snap peas
6-8 spring onions (white and light
    green parts only), cut into 1-cm/
    ½-inch pieces
Extra-virgin olive oil
Ground black pepper

2 large tuna steaks, each about
    500 g/1 lb and 2.5-cm/1-inch
    thick
1 teaspoon paprika
1 tablespoon finely chopped fresh dill
175 g/6 oz mixed baby salad leaves

1  Whisk the honey, mustard and vinegar in a small, non-reactive bowl. Slowly drizzle in the oil, whisking until the dressing is emulsified. Season with ½ teaspoon salt and set aside.

2  Prepare the grill for grilling/direct cooking over medium heat (180-230°C/ 350-450°F) (see pages 26-27) and preheat the grill pan on the cooking grates.

3  Spread the pecans in a single layer on the grill pan. Cook over **GRILLING/DIRECT MEDIUM HEAT** for 5-10 minutes, with the lid closed as much as possible and stirring once or twice, until they darken a shade and are fragrant. Wearing insulated barbecue gloves, carefully pour the nuts from the grill pan into a small bowl to cool (they will crisp as they cool) and place the grill pan back over grilling/direct heat.

4  Toss the sugar snap peas and spring onions with oil in a large bowl and season with salt and pepper. Arrange the vegetables in a single layer on the grill pan. Cook over **GRILLING/DIRECT MEDIUM HEAT** for 5-6 minutes, with the lid closed as much as possible and stirring occasionally, until the vegetables are slightly softened and charred. Wearing insulated barbecue gloves, remove the pan from the grill and transfer the vegetables to a salad bowl.

5  Season the tuna steaks evenly with the paprika, dill and salt and pepper. Place the soaked plank over **GRILLING/DIRECT MEDIUM HEAT** and close the lid. After 5-10 minutes, when the plank begins to smoke and char, place the tuna on the plank and cook over **GRILLING/DIRECT MEDIUM HEAT** for 12-15 minutes, with the lid closed, until the tuna is a little pink in the centre and is beginning to flake. Remove from the grill and cut into bite-sized pieces.

6  Put the salad leaves, pecans and tuna in the salad bowl with the vegetables. Pour the dressing over the salad, toss to mix and serve immediately.

# WOOD-GRILLED TUNA STEAKS
## WITH SMOKED FENNEL RELISH

**IDEAL GRILL:**

**SMOKE INTENSITY:** moderate

**PREP TIME:** 30 minutes

**COOKING TIME:** about 16 minutes

**SERVES:** 4

1 large fennel bulb, about 500g/
    1 lb
1 large red pepper
4 ripe plum tomatoes, halved
    lengthwise
Extra-virgin olive oil

2 large handfuls oak wood chips,
    soaked in water for at least 30
    minutes

2 tablespoons sherry vinegar
½ teaspoon smoked paprika
1 teaspoon sea salt
¾ teaspoon ground black pepper
50 g/2 oz/hazelnuts, toasted,
    skinned and coarsely chopped
15 g/½ oz fresh flat-leaf parsley,
    chopped

4 tuna steaks, each about 175 g/
    6 oz and 2.5 cm/1 inch thick

*To toast the hazelnuts, spread them on a baking sheet and bake for about 10 minutes in a preheated 180°C/350°F/Gas mark 4 oven, turning occasionally, until the skins are cracked and the nut flesh is toasted. Transfer to a clean tea towel and leave to cool for 5 minutes. Wrap the hazelnuts in the towel and rub them against each other to remove most of their papery skins. Don't worry if every last bit of skin doesn't come off.*

1 Prepare a two-zone fire for high heat (230–290°C/450–550°F) (see pages 20–22).

2 Cut off the thick stalks and the root end from the fennel bulb and discard. Cut the bulb in half lengthways and then cut away and remove the thick, triangular core. Cut the fennel vertically into 1-cm/½-inch slices. Cut off the top and bottom of the pepper. Make a cut down the side and open it up into a large strip. Remove the ribs and seeds. Brush the fennel slices and tomato halves with 1 tablespoon of oil.

3 Brush the cooking grate clean. Drain and add half of the wood chips to the charcoal and put the lid on the grill. When the wood begins to smoke, cook the fennel, pepper (shiny skin side down) and tomato halves (cut side down) over **GRILLING/DIRECT HIGH HEAT**, with the lid closed as much as possible. Cook the fennel until it is crisp-tender, about 8 minutes, turning once; the pepper until it is blackened and blistered, 6–8 minutes (do not turn); and the tomatoes until they are charred, about 6 minutes, turning once. Remove from the grill as they are done. Place the pepper strip in a bowl, cover with clingfilm to trap the steam and leave to stand for 5–10 minutes. Decrease the temperature of the grill to medium heat (180–230°C/350–450°F).

4 Remove the pepper from the bowl and peel away and discard the charred skin. Cut the fennel, pepper and tomatoes into 1-cm/½-inch pieces.

5 Whisk the vinegar, paprika, ½ teaspoon of the salt and ½ teaspoon of the pepper in a medium, non-reactive bowl. Gradually whisk in 4 tablespoons of oil. Add the fennel, pepper, tomatoes, hazelnuts and parsley to the bowl and mix. Set aside at room temperature.

6 Brush the tuna steaks on both sides with oil and season evenly with the remaining ½ teaspoon salt and the remaining ¼ teaspoon pepper. Brush the cooking grate clean. Drain and add the remaining wood chips to the charcoal and put the lid on the grill. When the wood begins to smoke, cook the tuna over **GRILLING/DIRECT MEDIUM HEAT** for about 8 minutes, with the lid closed as much as possible and turning once, until just turning opaque throughout. Remove from the grill and serve warm with the relish.

# LEMON-GARLIC SWORDFISH STEAKS
## WITH SMOKED PEPPERS AND ONIONS

**IDEAL GRILL:**

**SMOKE INTENSITY:** mild

**PREP TIME:** 20 minutes

**MARINATING TIME:** 1-2 hours

**COOKING TIME:** 18-22 minutes

**SPECIAL EQUIPMENT:** perforated grill pan

**SERVES:** 4

### MARINADE
4 tablespoons extra-virgin olive oil
1 tablespoon grated lemon zest
3 tablespoons fresh lemon juice
1 tablespoon finely chopped garlic
1 teaspoon sea salt
½ teaspoon dried thyme

4 swordfish steaks, each 250–
    300 g/8-10 oz and about 2.5 cm/
    1 inch thick

2 red peppers, cut into 5-mm/¼-inch
    slices
1 onion, halved and cut into 5-mm/
    ¼-inch slices
1 tablespoon extra-virgin olive oil
½ teaspoon sea salt
¼ teaspoon ground black pepper

1 large handful mesquite wood chips,
    soaked in water for at least
    30 minutes

1 tablespoon cider vinegar
75 g/3 oz pitted kalamata olives,
    each cut in half

*Take care not to overcook the fish, which should be moist and just beginning to flake when removed from the grill.*

**1** Whisk the marinade ingredients in a small bowl.

**2** Place the swordfish steaks in a shallow glass or china dish large enough to hold them in a single layer. Pour in the marinade, turning the swordfish to coat evenly. Cover with clingfilm and refrigerate for 1-2 hours.

**3** Prepare the grill for grilling/direct cooking over low heat (130–180°C/250–350°F) (see pages 26-27) and preheat the grill pan on the cooking grates.

**4** Combine the pepper and onion slices with the oil, salt and pepper in a medium bowl; carefully turn to coat.

**5** Drain and add the wood chips to the smoker box of a gas grill, following manufacturer's instructions, and close the lid. When the wood begins to smoke, arrange the vegetables in a single layer on the grill pan and cook over **GRILLING/ DIRECT LOW HEAT** for 10-12 minutes, with the lid closed as much as possible and turning occasionally, until slightly charred and softened. Wearing insulated barbecue gloves, remove the pan from the grill and transfer the vegetables to a small, non-reactive bowl. Stir in the vinegar and olives and set aside.

**6** Increase the temperature of the grill to high heat (230–290°C/450–550°F).

**7** Brush the cooking grates clean. Lift the swordfish from the dish and let the excess marinade drip back into the dish. Discard the marinade. Cook the swordfish over **GRILLING/DIRECT HIGH HEAT** for 8-10 minutes, with the lid closed as much as possible and turning once, until just opaque in the centre but still juicy. Transfer to individual plates or a serving plate and spoon the pepper and onion slices around the swordfish. Serve warm.

# PROSCIUTTO-WRAPPED TROUT
## WITH SPINACH-PINE NUT STUFFING

**IDEAL GRILL:**

**SMOKE INTENSITY:** mild

**PREP TIME:** 40 minutes

**COOKING TIME:** 12–16 minutes

**SERVES:** 4

## STUFFING

1 tablespoon extra-virgin olive oil

1 shallot, finely chopped

300 g/10 oz fresh baby spinach

50 g/2 oz fresh breadcrumbs

3 tablespoons chopped sultanas

2 tablespoons pine nuts, toasted

2 tablespoons finely grated
    Parmesan cheese

1 teaspoon finely chopped fresh
    rosemary

2 tablespoons dry white wine *or*
    dry vermouth

Sea salt

Ground black pepper

4 whole trout, each 375–425 g/
    12–14 oz, butterflied and deboned

16 thin Parma ham slices, about
    250 g/8 oz total weight

1 large handful maple or oak wood
    chips, soaked in water for at least
    30 minutes

1 lemon, quartered (optional)

*To toast the pine nuts, spread them in a medium frying pan over a medium heat, and cook for about 2 minutes, stirring occasionally, until lightly browned. Transfer to a plate to cool.*

1 Prepare a two-zone fire for medium heat (180–230°C/350–450°F) (see pages 20–22).

2 Heat the oil in a large frying pan over a medium heat. Add the shallot and cook for about 3 minutes, stirring occasionally, until softened. Add the spinach and cover. Cook for about 5 minutes, stirring occasionally, until the spinach is wilted and tender. Remove from the heat and leave to cool.

3 Roughly chop the spinach and place the chopped spinach with the shallot in a medium bowl. Mix in the breadcrumbs, sultanas, pine nuts, cheese and rosemary. Stir in the wine. Season with salt and pepper. Divide the spinach mixture between the trout, packing it evenly into the body cavities. Close the fish over the filling.

4 Overlap four pieces of Parma ham. Place a trout vertically along one short side of the prosciutto bed. Roll the trout with the ham, wrapping it up. Set aside and repeat with the remaining trout.

5 Brush the cooking grate clean. Drain and add the wood chips to the charcoal and put the lid on the grill. When the wood begins to smoke, cook the trout, with the seam side of the ham down first, over **GRILLING/DIRECT MEDIUM HEAT** for 12–16 minutes, with the lid closed as much as possible and turning once, until the Parma ham is crisp and the trout is cooked through. Remove from the grill and serve immediately with lemon quarters, if preferred.

# SMOKED HERRING AND ONIONS

**IDEAL GRILL:**

**SMOKE INTENSITY:** moderate

**PREP TIME:** 20 minutes

**COOKING TIME:** 5–12 minutes

**SERVES:** 4

8 herring, each about 150 g/5 oz, cleaned

2 large onions, cut crossways into 8-mm/⅓-inch slices

Vegetable oil

2 large handfuls apple wood chips, soaked in water for at least 30 minutes

4 slices dark rye bread

Wholegrain Dijon mustard

Sour cream

Fresh flat-leaf parsley

*The fish are butterflied, not filleted, which is an important distinction. They have two flaps of fillets attached at the bottom by the tail. If cut into two fillets, they will cook too quickly.*

1 Prepare a two-zone fire for medium heat (180–230°C/350–450°F) (see pages 20–22).

2 Butterfly the herring and remove the heads and central bones. Leave the tails attached. Lightly brush the herring and onion slices on both sides with oil.

3 Brush the cooking grate clean. Drain and add the wood chips to the charcoal and put the lid on the grill. When the wood begins to smoke, cook the herring, skin side down, over **ROASTING/INDIRECT MEDIUM HEAT** for 5–10 minutes depending on the thickness of the fillets, with the lid closed (do not turn), until cooked through. At the same time, cook the onion slices over **GRILLING/DIRECT MEDIUM HEAT** for 8–12 minutes, turning once or twice, until tender and nicely browned. Remove from the grill as they are done.

4 Serve the herring and onions on dark rye bread slices with mustard and soured cream to spread on the bread as liked. Top with parsley.

# ROSEMARY-SMOKED WHOLE SEA BASS
## WITH GREEK COUNTRY SALAD

**IDEAL GRILL:**

**SMOKE INTENSITY:** moderate

**PREP TIME:** 30 minutes

**STANDING TIME:** 30 minutes–2 hours

**COOKING TIME:** about 15 minutes

**SPECIAL EQUIPMENT:** kitchen string

**SERVES:** 4

*The easiest way to tell if fish is fresh is to ask to smell it. It should smell like the sea at high tide on a spring morning.*

2 whole sea bass, each about 625 g/1¼ lb, cleaned, gutted, scaled, gills and all fins removed
3 lemons
2 tablespoons extra-virgin olive oil
Sea salt
Ground black pepper
10 rosemary sprigs, each about 15 cm/6 inches long

### SALAD
4 tablespoons extra-virgin olive oil
2 ripe plum tomatoes, deseeded and chopped
1 cucumber, chopped
1 small green pepper, chopped
½ red onion, finely chopped
20 pitted kalamata olives, roughly chopped

1 Cut three or four parallel slashes about 1 cm/½ inch deep and 2.5 cm/1 inch apart on each side of the fish. Cut one of the lemons in half crossways. Squeeze 2 tablespoons of juice into a medium, non-reactive bowl and set aside for the salad. Cut the other two lemons into thin slices. Set aside the slices of one lemon to serve with the smoked sea bass. The slices of the other lemon will be used inside the fish.

2 Lightly brush each fish with the oil and season evenly, inside and outside, with salt and pepper. Place half the lemon slices from one lemon, and one rosemary sprig, cut in half, inside the cavity of each fish. Tie each fish across with kitchen string in two or three places to hold it closed. Refrigerate the fish while you preheat the grill. Soak the remaining eight rosemary sprigs in water for at least 30 minutes.

3 Pour 4 tablespoons oil into the bowl with the reserved lemon juice and whisk to combine. Add the remaining salad ingredients and mix well. Season with salt and pepper. Leave to stand at room temperature for at least 30 minutes. If liked, to fully incorporate the flavours, leave the salad to sit at room temperature for up to 2 hours.

4 Prepare a two-zone fire for medium heat (180–230°C/350–450°F) (see pages 20–22).

5 Brush the cooking grate clean. Drain and add the rosemary sprigs to the charcoal and put the lid on the grill. When the sprigs begin to smoke, cook the sea bass over **GRILLING/DIRECT MEDIUM HEAT** for about 15 minutes, with the lid closed as much as possible, using a metal spatula to carefully turn once (do not be concerned if the skin sticks to the cooking grate), until the flesh is opaque near the bone but still juicy. Remove from the grill.

6 To serve, carefully remove the string from the fish and then cut off the heads and tails. Cut along the backbone and then open the fish like a book. Remove the bones and lift the flesh off the skin. Serve alongside the salad with the lemon slices.

# Vegetables and Sides

# GRILL-ROASTED ARTICHOKES
## WITH SMOKED GARLIC AIOLI

**IDEAL GRILL:**

**SMOKE INTENSITY:** moderate

**PREP TIME:** 30 minutes

**COOKING TIME:** about 47 minutes

**SERVES:** 6

*Choose artichokes that are compact and heavy for their size, and that squeak when their leaves are squeezed together.*

1 lemon
6 artichokes, each 200–250 g/
    7–8 oz
2 garlic bulbs
2 tablespoons plus 1 teaspoon extra-
    virgin olive oil
1 teaspoon water
Sea salt
Ground black pepper

2 large handfuls oak wood chips,
    soaked in water for at least
    30 minutes

240 ml/8 fl oz mayonnaise
2 tablespoons chopped fresh flat-leaf
    parsley

1 Prepare a two-zone fire for medium heat (180–230°C/350–450°F) (see pages 20–22).

2 Cut the lemon in half and squeeze the juice into a large, non-reactive bowl; fill the bowl two-thirds full with water. Reserve the lemon halves. Working with one artichoke at a time, trim the very end of the stalk (if attached) and remove the smallest leaves. Using scissors, snip off the thorny tips from the outer leaves. As you work, rub the cut surfaces with the pulp side of the lemon halves. Put the trimmed artichokes in the lemon water.

3 Cut off the tops of the garlic bulbs to expose the cloves; discard the tops. Place the garlic bulbs side by side on a square of aluminium foil. Wrap the foil round the garlic, like a canoe, leaving the tops exposed. Drizzle with 1 teaspoon of the oil and 1 teaspoon water and season with a pinch of salt and pepper.

4 Drain the artichokes. Place each artichoke on a square of aluminium foil. Drizzle the remaining 2 tablespoons of oil over the artichokes and season them evenly with 1½ teaspoons salt and ¼ teaspoon pepper. Wrap each artichoke in its foil.

5 Brush the cooking grate clean. Drain and add one handful of the wood chips to the charcoal and put the lid on the grill. When the wood begins to smoke, cook the garlic and artichokes over ROASTING/INDIRECT MEDIUM HEAT for about 40 minutes, with the lid closed as much as possible. Remove the garlic from the grill and leave to cool slightly.

6 Open the foil to expose the artichokes. Drain and add the second handful of wood chips to the charcoal. Continue grilling the artichokes for about 7 minutes more, turning the artichokes over once in the foil, until a large leaf can easily be pulled off. Remove the artichokes from the grill.

7 Squeeze out the garlic cloves into a medium bowl. Mash the garlic with a fork. Add the mayonnaise and parsley and mix. Season with salt and pepper. Serve the artichokes warm or at room temperature with the aioli.

# SUMMER VEGETABLE SUCCOTASH

IDEAL GRILL:

PREP TIME: 15 minutes

COOKING TIME: 8-12 minutes

SERVES: 8

3 courgettes, ends trimmed, each cut in half lengthways

2 tablespoons extra-virgin olive oil

2 fresh corn cobs, outer leaves and silk removed

1 large red pepper

½ red onion, finely chopped

¾ teaspoon sea salt

2 teaspoons finely chopped garlic

300 g/10 oz frozen broad beans, thawed

2 tablespoons finely chopped fresh oregano or basil

¼ teaspoon ground black pepper

1 Prepare a two-zone fire for medium heat (180–230°C/350–450°F) (see pages 20–22).

2 Brush the cooking grate clean. Brush the courgettes with 1 tablespoon of the oil. Cook the courgettes, corn and pepper over GRILLING/DIRECT MEDIUM HEAT, with the lid closed as much as possible, until the courgettes are crisp-tender, the corn is browned in spots and tender, and the pepper is blackened and blistered all over, turning occasionally. The courgettes will take about 6 minutes, and the corn and the pepper will take 10–12 minutes. Remove from the grill as they are done. Put the pepper in a bowl, cover with clingfilm to trap the steam, and leave to stand for about 10 minutes.

3 When the vegetables are cool enough to handle, remove and discard the stalk end, skin and seeds from the pepper and cut the pepper and courgettes into 1-cm/½-inch peices. Cut the kernels off the corn cobs.

4 Warm the remaining 1 tablespoon oil in a large frying pan over medium heat. Add the onion and ¼ teaspoon of the salt and cook for about 4 minutes, stirring occasionally, until tender. Stir in the garlic and cook for about 1 minute until fragrant. Add the broad beans, courgettes, corn and pepper. Cover and cook for about 3 minutes, stirring occasionally, until heated through. Stir in the oregano, the remaining ½ teaspoon salt and the pepper. Serve immediately.

*Any kind of fresh summer bean can be used instead of the frozen broad beans. Cook in boiling water for about 5 minutes until just tender. Drain and rinse under cold running water.*

# ASPARAGUS AND PANCETTA
## WITH LEMON-TARRAGON VINAIGRETTE

IDEAL
GRILL:

SMOKE INTENSITY: mild

PREP TIME: 15 minutes

COOKING TIME: 6-8 minutes

SERVES: 4-6

*Choose asparagus spears about as thick as your finger, as they are better on the grill than pencil-thin spears.*

75 g/3 oz pancetta *or* 2 rashers thick-
    cut bacon, chopped
1 kg/2 lb asparagus
Extra-virgin olive oil
Sea salt
Ground black pepper

### VINAIGRETTE
1 tablespoon finely grated lemon zest
2 tablespoons fresh lemon juice
2 tablespoons white wine vinegar
1 tablespoon finely chopped shallot
2 teaspoons finely chopped fresh
    tarragon
1 teaspoon runny honey

1 small handful hickory wood chips,
    soaked in water for at least
    30 minutes

1 Cook the pancetta pieces in a small frying pan over a medium heat for 4-6 minutes, stirring occasionally, until crisp and browned. Drain on kitchen paper.

2 Prepare a two-zone fire for medium heat (180-230°C/350-450°F) (see pages 20-22).

3 Remove and discard the tough bottom of each asparagus spear by grasping at each end and bending it gently until the spear snaps at its natural point of tenderness, usually about two-thirds of the way down the spear. Drizzle the spears with oil and lightly season with salt and pepper.

4 Whisk the vinaigrette ingredients in a small, non-reactive bowl. Slowly add 4 tablespoons oil and whisk until the vinaigrette is emulsified. Season with salt and pepper.

5 Brush the cooking grate clean. Drain and add the wood chips to the charcoal and put the lid on the grill. When the wood begins to smoke, cook the asparagus over GRILLING/DIRECT MEDIUM HEAT for 6-8 minutes, with the lid closed as much as possible and turning occasionally, until tender.

6 Transfer the asparagus to a serving plate, drizzle with the vinaigrette and top with the pancetta. Serve warm or at room temperature.

# CHICKPEA AND MOZZARELLA SALAD
## WITH SMOKED AUBERGINE AND TOMATOES

IDEAL GRILL:

SMOKE INTENSITY: mild

PREP TIME: 30 minutes

COOKING TIME: 15–20 minutes

COOLING TIME: about 30 minutes

MARINATING TIME: at least 1 hour

SERVES: 4–6

*The chickpeas will absorb liquid and smoke from the aubergine and tomatoes while the salad marinates. Serve as a side dish or as a vegetarian main course.*

### VINAIGRETTE
2 teaspoons finely grated lime zest
4 tablespoons fresh lime juice
4 tablespoons extra-virgin olive oil
1 teaspoon finely chopped garlic
½ teaspoon ground cumin
¼ teaspoon ground cayenne pepper

Sea salt
Ground black pepper

4 plum tomatoes, each halved
    lengthways
1 large rounded aubergine, about
    500 g/1 lb, ends trimmed, halved
    lengthways
3–4 spring onions, ends trimmed

1 large handful mesquite wood chips,
    soaked in water for at least
    30 minutes
2 x 475-g/15-oz cans chickpeas,
    rinsed
250-g/8 oz mozzarella cheese, cut
    into 5-mm/¼-inch cubes
4 tablespoons roughly chopped fresh
    flat-leaf parsley

1  Prepare the grill for grilling/direct cooking over low heat (130–180°C/250–350°F) (see pages 26–27).

2  Whisk the vinaigrette ingredients in a small, non-reactive bowl. Season with salt and pepper. Lightly brush the vegetables with some of the vinaigrette. Reserve the remaining vinaigrette.

3  Brush the cooking grates clean. Drain and add the wood chips to the smoker box of a gas grill, following manufacturer's instructions, and close the lid. When the wood begins to smoke, place the vegetables over GRILLING/DIRECT LOW HEAT, close the lid, and cook until the vegetables are tender and the tomato and aubergine skins wrinkle and start to brown, turning occasionally. The aubergine will take 15–20 minutes, the tomatoes will take 10–15 minutes and the spring onions will take about 10 minutes. Remove from the grill as they are done.

4  Place the tomatoes and aubergine in a large, non-reactive bowl and leave to cool for about 30 minutes (during this time, the tomatoes and aubergine will release some liquid). After the aubergine and tomatoes have cooled, transfer them to a chopping board; reserve the liquid. Cut all of the vegetables into bite-sized pieces. Put the vegetables back in the bowl with the liquid and add the chickpeas, cheese and the reserved vinaigrette. Toss to coat. Set aside at room temperature for at least 1 hour, or in the refrigerator for up to 8 hours.

5  Before serving, mix in the parsley and season with salt and pepper. Served chilled or at room temperature.

# VEGETABLE BULGAR SALAD
## WITH FETA AND MINT

IDEAL
GRILL:

SMOKE INTENSITY: mild

PREP TIME: 15 minutes, plus
about 30 minutes to soak
the bulgar

COOKING TIME: 12–15 minutes

STANDING TIME: at least
30 minutes

SERVES: 6–8

300 g/10 oz bulgar wheat
300 ml/10 fl oz boiling water

VINAIGRETTE
40 g/1½ oz fresh mint, roughly
    chopped
3 tablespoons cider vinegar
2 teaspoons Dijon mustard
1 garlic clove, finely chopped

Extra-virgin olive oil
Sea salt
Ground black pepper

2 portobello mushrooms, each
    about 125 g/4 oz, stalks and gills
    removed
2 medium courgettes, about 375 g/
    12 oz total weight, ends trimmed,
    each cut in half lengthways
2 red peppers, about 375 g/12 oz
    total weight, each cut into
    4 pieces

3 large handfuls apple wood chips,
    soaked in water for at least
    30 minutes

375 g/12 oz cherry tomatoes, each
    cut into quarters
125 g/4 oz feta cheese, crumbled
15 g/½ oz roughly chopped fresh
    flat-leaf parsley

1 Mix the bulgar with the boiling water in a large, non-reactive bowl and leave to
soak for about 30 minutes until the water is absorbed.

2 Prepare the grill for grilling/direct cooking over low heat (130–180°C/250–350°F)
(see pages 26–27).

3 Combine the vinaigrette ingredients In a small bowl. Whisk in 75 ml/3 fl oz oil and
season with 1 teaspoon salt and ½ teaspoon pepper. Pour the vinaigrette over
the bulgar and toss to coat.

4 Lightly brush the mushrooms, courgettes, and peppers with oil and season evenly
with salt and pepper.

5 Brush the cooking grates clean. Drain and add the wood chips to the smoker box
of a gas grill, following manufacturer's instructions, and close the lid. When the
wood begins to smoke, cook the vegetables over GRILLING/DIRECT LOW HEAT for
12–15 minutes with the lid closed as much as possible and turning occasionally,
until crisp-tender and lightly charred. Remove from the grill as they are done.

6 Cut the vegetables into 1-cm/½-inch pieces and add to the bulgar. Gently fold in
the tomatoes, cheese and parsley. Set the salad aside at room temperature for
at least 30 minutes, or cover and refrigerate for up to 24 hours. Serve at room
temperature.

*This salad is better the next day because the smokiness deepens as the
ingredients mellow.*

# SMOKED ARTICHOKE PASTA
## WITH LEMONY VINAIGRETTE

IDEAL
GRILL:

**SMOKE INTENSITY:** mild

**PREP TIME:** 25 minutes

**COOKING TIME:** 10–12 minutes

**SPECIAL EQUIPMENT:** perforated
grill pan

**SERVES:** 6–8

### DRESSING
4 tablespoons fresh lemon juice
40 g/1½ oz kalamata olives, finely
chopped
1 teaspoon finely chopped fresh
thyme
120 ml/4 fl oz extra-virgin olive oil
Sea salt
Ground black pepper

3 peppers, preferably 1 red, 1 yellow
and 1 orange, each cut into
5-mm/¼-inch strips
2 x 425-g/14-oz cans artichoke
hearts (not in marinade) *or* 12
frozen artichoke hearts, thawed,
drained and quartered
4 tablespoons extra-virgin olive oil
2 teaspoons finely chopped garlic

1 large handful hickory or oak wood
chips, soaked in water for at least
30 minutes

250 g/8 oz dried penne
250 g/8 oz mozzarella cheese, cut
into 5-mm/¼-inch cubes

*To achieve the best possible browning of the artichokes, drain off as much liquid*
*as possible and coat them evenly with oil.*

1 Prepare the grill for grilling/direct cooking over medium heat (180–230°C/350–
450°F) (see pages 26–27) and preheat the grill pan on the cooking grates.

2 Whisk the lemon juice, olives and thyme in a large, non-reactive serving bowl.
Slowly drizzle and whisk in 120 ml/4 fl oz oil until it is emulsified. Season with salt
and pepper. Set aside.

3 Mix the peppers and artichokes with 4 tablespoons oil and the garlic in a
large bowl.

4 Drain and add the wood chips to the smoker box of a gas grill, following
manufacturer's instructions, and close the lid. When the wood begins to smoke,
arrange the peppers and artichokes in a single layer on the grill pan. Cook over
**GRILLING/DIRECT MEDIUM HEAT** for 10–12 minutes, with the lid closed as much as
possible and turning occasionally, until slightly charred and softened. Wearing
insulated barbecue gloves, remove the pan from the grill and set it on a heatproof
surface. Transfer the vegetables to the large serving bowl with the dressing.

5 Cook the pasta in a large saucepan of boiling, salted water according to packet
directions. Drain the pasta and add to the serving bowl. Add the cheese and toss
to combine. Serve warm or at room temperature.

# SMOKED MARINATED TOFU
## WITH CHINESE CABBAGE SLAW

IDEAL
GRILL:

SMOKE INTENSITY: strong

PREP TIME: 20 minutes

MARINATING TIME: 1–2 hours

COOKING TIME: about 2 hours

SERVES: 6

*Do not use silken tofu or even firm tofu for this recipe. Only extra-firm tofu will be able to sit on the cooking grate for two hours without falling apart.*

3 x 425g–500 g/14–16 oz packets
      extra-firm tofu, drained
6 tablespoons soy sauce
6 tablespoons rice vinegar
3 tablespoons fish sauce

4 fist-sized hickory wood chunks

6 tablespoons rapeseed oil
2 teaspoons granulated sugar
1 teaspoon hot chilli paste
2 tablespoons toasted sesame oil
1 small head Chinese leaves, about
      1 kg/2¼ pounds, cored and
      thinly sliced
2 peppers, 1 red and 1 yellow, cut into
      very thin strips
4 spring onions (white and light
      green parts only), thinly sliced
Sea salt

1 Cut each tofu block in half horizontally to make six rectangular slabs. Whisk 3 tablespoons of the soy sauce, 3 tablespoons of the vinegar and the fish sauce in a large glass or china baking dish large enough to hold the tofu in a single layer. Add the tofu and turn to coat. Refrigerate for 1–2 hours, basting occasionally.

2 Prepare the smoker for roasting/indirect cooking with very low heat (95–130°C/ 200–250°F) (see pages 23–25). When the temperature reaches 110°C/225°F, add two wood chunks to the charcoal.

3 Remove the tofu from the marinade and pat dry with kitchen paper. Brush the tofu with 2 tablespoons of the rapeseed oil. Brush the cooking grate clean. Smoke the tofu over ROASTING/INDIRECT VERY LOW HEAT for about 2 hours, with the lid closed, until it is a light mahogany brown. Add the remaining two wood chunks to the charcoal after the first hour. Add more lit briquettes as necessary to maintain a steady heat.

4 Meanwhile, whisk the remaining 3 tablespoons soy sauce and vinegar, the sugar and the hot chilli paste in a large, non-reactive bowl. Gradually whisk in the remaining rapeseed oil and the sesame oil. Add the Chinese leaves, peppers and spring onions and mix well. Cover and refrigerate for up to 1 hour before serving. Season with salt.

5 Remove the tofu from the smoker. Serve warm with the slaw.

# THREE BEAN AND CHORIZO CHILLI

**PREP TIME:** 20 minutes, plus about 55 minutes to simmer the chilli

**SPECIAL EQUIPMENT:** 5-litre/ 8-pint cast-iron casserole

**SERVES:** 6

250 g/8 oz smoked chorizo sausage, cut into 1-cm/½-inch cubes
1 tablespoon extra-virgin olive oil
1 large onion, finely chopped
1 large green pepper, cut into 1-cm/ ½-inch pieces
1 serrano *or* jalapeño chilli pepper, deseeded and finely chopped
1 tablespoon finely chopped garlic
3 tablespoons prepared chilli seasoning
2 teaspoons ground cumin
2 teaspoons dried oregano
2 x 425 g/14-oz cans chopped tomatoes
350 ml/12 fl oz lager
2 x 475 g/15-oz cans pinto beans, rinsed
475 g/15-oz can red kidney beans, rinsed
475 g/15-oz can chickpeas, rinsed
¾ teaspoon sea salt
Soured cream (optional)
Grated Cheddar cheese (optional)
Hot pepper sauce (optional)

1 Cook the chorizo with the oil in a 5-litre/8-pint cast-iron casserole over a medium heat for about 5 minutes, stirring occasionally, until the chorizo begins to brown. Add the onion, bell pepper, chilli pepper and garlic. Cook for about 5 minutes, stirring occasionally, until the onion is tender.

2 Add the chilli seasoning, cumin and oregano and stir for 15 seconds. Add the tomatoes and lager and stir well. Add all the beans and bring to a simmer. Reduce the heat to medium-low and simmer for about 45 minutes, stirring occasionally, until the juices have thickened. Remove from the heat and season with the salt. Serve hot with soured cream, cheese and hot pepper sauce, if liked.

*This chilli is an excellent side dish for the Barbecued Brisket Tamales (see page 89), but it can also be served as a main course.*

# CIDER AND BACON BEANS

IDEAL
GRILL:

PREP TIME: 15 minutes

COOKING TIME: about 1¼ hours

SPECIAL EQUIPMENT: 3-litre/5-
pint cast-iron caserole

SERVES: 8

750 ml/1¼ pints fresh apple cider
3 tablespoons soft light brown sugar
75 ml/3 fl oz tomato ketchup
2 tablespoons spicy brown mustard
1 tablespoon Worcestershire sauce
4 bacon rashers, cut into 2.5-cm/
    1-inch pieces
1 large onion, finely chopped
4 x 475-g/15-oz cans cannellini
    beans, rinsed
Sea salt
Ground black pepper

*These beans are delicious on their own, but if you are a real smoke fanatic, smoke the beans with a wood that complements the bacon. For example, if you have used bacon smoked with apple wood, then use apple wood chips, or hickory wood chips for bacon that has been smoked with hickory.*

1 Prepare the grill for grilling/direct and roasting/indirect cooking over low heat (130–180°C/250–350°F) (see pages 26–27).

2 Bring the cider to the boil in a medium saucepan over high heat. Cook for about 10 minutes until reduced to 350 ml/12 fl oz. Add the brown sugar, ketchup, mustard and Worcestershire sauce and whisk until the sugar is dissolved. Set aside.

3 Place a 3-litre/5-pint cast-iron casserole over GRILLING/DIRECT LOW HEAT, add the bacon and cook for 10–12 minutes, stirring occasionally, until crisp and browned. Add the onion and cook for 6–8 minutes, stirring occasionally, until golden. Add the beans and the cider mixture and stir well. Bring to a simmer. Slide the casserole over ROASTING/INDIRECT LOW HEAT and cook for 45–50 minutes, uncovered, with the grill lid closed, until the cooking liquid has reduced by about half. Remove from the grill and leave to stand for about 5 minutes. Season with salt and pepper and serve warm.

# ROASTED PEPPER MACARONI CHEESE

**IDEAL GRILL:**

**PREP TIME:** 20 minutes

**COOKING TIME:** 30–42 minutes

**SPECIAL EQUIPMENT:** 5-litre/ 8-pint cast-iron casserole

**SERVES:** 6–8

75 g/3 oz unsalted butter

4 mild chillies

3 red peppers

40 g/1½ oz plain flour

750 ml/1¼ pints full-fat milk, heated

450 g/14½ oz mature Cheddar cheese, grated

1½ teaspoons sea salt

½ teaspoon hot pepper sauce

500 g/1 lb dried short-cut macaroni

2 large eggs

*If poblano chillies are unavailable, use an ordinary pepper and a serrano or jalapeño chilli. Here's how: deseed and chop 1 large green pepper and 1 or 2 serrano or jalapeño chillies. Warm 2 tablespoons extra-virgin olive oil in a small frying pan over a medium heat. Sauté the peppers and chillies for about 5 minutes, stirring occasionally, until tender. Stir into the sauce with the cheese.*

1 Prepare the grill for grilling/direct and roasting/indirect cooking over medium heat (180–230°C/350–450°F) (see pages 26–27).

2 Grease a 5-litre/8-pint cast-iron casserole with 15 g/½ oz butter.

3 Brush the cooking grates clean. Grill the peppers over GRILLING/DIRECT MEDIUM HEAT for 10–12 minutes, with the lid closed as much as possible and turning occasionally, until blackened and blistered all over. Put in a bowl, cover with clingfilm to trap the steam and leave to stand for about 10 minutes. When cool enough to handle, remove and discard the stalk ends, skin and seeds. Cut into 1-cm/½-inch pieces.

4 Melt the remaining butter in a large saucepan over a medium-low heat. Whisk in the flour and let bubble for 1 minute, without browning. Whisk in the hot milk and bring to a simmer over a medium heat, whisking often. Remove from the heat. Add 400 g/13 oz of the cheese to the saucepan and stir until the cheese melts. Add the chopped chillies and peppers. Season with the salt and hot pepper sauce.

5 Cook the macaroni for about 3 minutes in a large saucepan of boiling, salted water (it will be undercooked). Drain and return the macaroni to its saucepan.

6 Whisk the eggs in a medium bowl. Gradually whisk in 240 ml/8 fl oz of the hot cheese mixture, and then stir the egg mixture back into the saucepan. Pour over the macaroni and stir well. Spread in the prepared casserole. Top with the remaining cheese. Cook over ROASTING/INDIRECT MEDIUM HEAT for for 20–30 minutes, with the lid closed, until bubbling. Remove from the grill and leave to rest for 5 minutes. Serve warm.

# WARM POTATO AND BACON SALAD
## WITH WHOLEGRAIN MUSTARD DRESSING

**PREP TIME:** 30 minutes, plus about 25 minutes for the potatoes

**SERVES:** 6

*Be sure to use waxy boiling potatoes with a thin, edible skin for this potato salad. They will hold together better than baking potatoes when tossed with the dressing.*

3 1.5 kg/3 lb red skinned potatoes, scrubbed
6 bacon rashers, cut into 2.5-cm/ 1-inch pieces
Rapeseed oil
200 ml/7 fl oz water
75 ml/3 fl oz cider vinegar
2 tablespoons wholegrain mustard
1 tablespoon granulated sugar
Sea salt
Ground black pepper
4 spring onions, finely sliced, white and green parts separated
1 tablespoon plain flour
2 tablespoons finely chopped fresh flat-leaf parsley

1 Put the potatoes in a large saucepan and cover with lightly salted water. Cover and bring to the boil over a high heat. Reduce the heat to medium and set the saucepan lid ajar. Cook for about 25 minutes until the potatoes are just tender. Drain and rinse under cold running water. Set aside while making the dressing.

2 Cook the bacon with 1 tablespoon oil for 8–10 minutes, stirring occasionally, until the bacon is crisp and browned. Using a slotted spoon, transfer the bacon to a plate lined with kitchen paper. Measure the bacon fat: you should have 3 tablespoons. If not, add more rapeseed oil. Set the frying pan aside.

3 Whisk the water, vinegar, mustard, sugar, 1 teaspoon salt and ¼ teaspoon pepper in a small, non-reactive bowl until the sugar and salt are dissolved. Set aside. Cut the potatoes into 5-mm/¼-inch slices. Remove the potato skins, if liked.

4 Return the pan with the bacon fat to a medium heat. Add the white parts of the spring onions and cook for about 2 minutes, stirring occasionally, until wilted. Sprinkle with the flour and stir well. Whisk in the vinegar mixture and bring to a simmer. Reduce the heat to very low and simmer for about 2 minutes until the flour taste has disappeared. Remove from the heat and add the potato slices, bacon, the green parts of the spring onions and the parsley and toss gently to coat with the dressing. Season with salt and pepper. Serve warm.

# FRESH CUCUMBER SALAD
## WITH SOURED CREAM AND DILL DRESSING

**PREP TIME:** 15 minutes

**DRAINING TIME:** 1–3 hours

**CHILLING TIME:** at least 2 hours

**SERVES:** 6–8

4 large cucumbers, seeds removed,
    cut into 5-mm/¼-inch half-moons

2¼ teaspoons sea salt

240/8 fl oz soured cream

3 tablespoons finely chopped
    fresh dill

3 tablespoons cider vinegar

1 teaspoon granulated sugar

¼ teaspoon ground black pepper

1 small red onion, thinly sliced

*This salad is a great way for
using up a glut of summer
cucumbers.*

*Salt draws the excess water from the cucumbers and keeps them crisp in the
dressing. Don't skip this step. Be sure to rinse the cucumber slices well to remove
the salt before adding to the dressing.*

1  Toss the cucumbers in a colander with 2 teaspoons of the salt. Leave to stand in
the sink to drain for at least 1 hour or up to 3 hours. Rinse well under cold running
water and pat dry with kitchen paper.

2  Whisk the soured cream, dill, vinegar, sugar, the remaining ¼ teaspoon salt and
the pepper in a medium, non-reactive bowl. Add the cucumbers and onion and
mix well. Cover and refrigerate for at least 2 hours or up to 2 days. Serve chilled.

# SWEET AND TANGY VEGETABLE SLAW

**PREP TIME:** 20 minutes

**CHILLING TIME:** about 2 hours

**SERVES:** 8–10

*A food processor fitted with a slicing blade makes very quick work of preparing the cabbage, cucumber, onion and peppers. Switch to the grating blade for the carrots.*

75 ml/3 fl oz cider vinegar
75 ml/3 fl oz rapeseed oil
75 g/3 oz granulated sugar
1 tablespoon sea salt
1½ teaspoons celery seeds
½ teaspoon ground black pepper

625 g/1¼ lb thinly sliced white
    cabbage
1 cucumber, cut into thin half-moons
100 g/3½ carrots, grated
200 g/7 oz sweet onions,
    thinly sliced
175 g/6 oz red pepper, thinly sliced
175 g/6 oz green pepper, thinly sliced

**1** Whisk the vinegar, oil, sugar, salt, celery seeds and pepper in a large, non-reactive bowl until the sugar and salt are dissolved. Add all the vegetables and mix well. Cover and refrigerate for about 2 hours until chilled. To blend the flavours even more, you can refrigerate the slaw for up to 1 day.

**2** Before serving, drain the slaw in a colander. Serve chilled.

*Like most slaws, this one will wilt and the volume will decrease as the marinating time increases. If you like tender slaw, leave it to marinate overnight.*

# CLASSIC COLESLAW

PREP TIME: 15 minutes

STANDING TIME: 30 minutes

SERVES: 6

1 white cabbage, about 1 kg/2 lb,
    thinly sliced
4 carrots, grated
1 tablespoon sea salt
150 ml/¼ pint mayonnaise
2 tablespoons sherry vinegar *or*
    cider vinegar
1 tablespoon granulated sugar
1 tablespoon Dijon mustard
1 teaspoon ground black pepper

*To avoid soggy coleslaw, remove as much water from the cabbage and carrots as you can. Do this by first salting the vegetables and letting them stand for 30 minutes. Then rinse the vegetables and squeeze them one handful at a time before adding the dressing.*

1 Toss the cabbage and carrots with the salt in a large bowl and leave to stand for 30 minutes.

2 Drain the cabbage and carrots in a colander and rinse well under cold running water. One handful at a time, squeeze the cabbage mixture to remove excess liquid and return to the bowl.

3 Whisk the mayonnaise, vinegar, sugar, mustard and pepper in a small bowl. Stir into the cabbage mixture. Serve immediately.

# GARLIC SPOONBREAD

IDEAL
GRILL:

PREP TIME: 20 minutes

COOKING TIME: about 35 minutes

SPECIAL EQUIPMENT: 25-cm/
10-inch cast-iron frying pan

SERVES: 8

65 g/2½ oz unsalted butter
1 tablespoon finely chopped garlic
750 ml/1¼ pints full-fat milk
1 teaspoon sea salt
¼ teaspoon ground black pepper
175 g/6 oz stone-ground yellow
    polenta
75 g/3 oz mature Cheddar cheese,
    grated
3 large eggs, separated, at room
    temperature

*The easily adjusted, steady heat of a gas grill is best for cooking the spoonbread.*

1 Prepare the grill for roasting/indirect cooking over medium heat (180–230°C/ 350–450°F) (see pages 26–27), keeping the temperature as close to 190°C/ 375°F as possible.

2 Grease a 25-cm/10-inch cast-iron frying pan with 15 g/½ oz of the butter.

3 Melt 15 g/½ oz of the remaining butter in a medium, heavy saucepan over a medium heat. Add the garlic and cook for about 2 minutes, stirring often, until it is softened but not browned. Add the milk, salt and pepper and bring to a simmer. Add the polenta and return to a simmer, whisking constantly. Reduce the heat to medium-low and simmer for about 2 minutes, whisking occasionally, until very thick. Remove from the heat, add the remaining butter and whisk until blended. Add the cheese and whisk until melted.

4 Beat the egg yolks in a medium bowl. Gradually beat in 120 ml/4 fl oz of the hot polenta mixture, and then stir the egg mixture back into the saucepan. Using an electric mixer set on high speed, beat the egg whites in a medium bowl until soft peaks form. Stir about a quarter of the egg whites into the polenta mixture, and then fold in the remaining egg whites with a rubber spatula. Spread in the prepared frying pan.

5 Grill over ROASTING/INDIRECT MEDIUM HEAT for about 35 minutes, with the lid closed, until the spoonbread has puffed evenly and is golden brown. Remove from the grill and serve immediately.

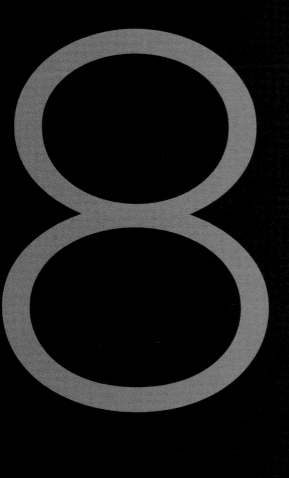

# Resources

# SAFETY

## GRILL SAFETY

Please read your owner's guide and familiarize yourself with and follow all 'dangers', 'warnings' and 'cautions'. Also follow the grilling procedures and maintenance requirements listed in your owner's guide.

If you cannot locate the owner's guide for your grill model, please contact the manufacturer prior to use. If you have any questions concerning the 'dangers', 'warnings' and 'cautions' contained in your Weber® gas or charcoal grill owner's guide, or if you do not have an owner's guide for your specific grill model, please contact Weber-Stephen Products LLC Customer Service, before using your grill. You can also access your owner's guide online at www.weber.com.

## BASIC FOOD SAFETY

Follow these basic rules to make sure your meal is as safe as it is tasty:

### 1 AVOID THE 'DANGER ZONE'.
If meat sits between 4 and 60°C/40 and 140°F ('the danger zone') for too long, unwelcome bacteria start to grow. So don't let it sit out on the worktop for extended periods of time – 20 minutes is fine; 2 hours is not. And after dinner, don't let smoked meat sit out on the table for hours. Wrap it up and refrigerate it. Besides, leftovers are among smoking's best rewards.

### 2 WASH AND CLEAN ANYTHING THAT TOUCHED RAW MEAT.
Never set a cooked piece of meat back on a chopping board that held it raw without first washing the board with soap and hot water. The same goes for knives, tongs and other tools.

### 3 NEVER USE A MEAT MARINADE IMMEDIATELY AS A SAUCE.
Pour the marinade into a saucepan and bring to the boil before you serve it to anyone. This will kill any harmful bacteria.

### 4 THAW FROZEN MEAT SLOWLY IN THE REFRIGERATOR.
It's also safe to thaw meat in cold water (which is faster), provided that you seal the meat in a plastic bag, you submerge the bag in the cold water and you change the water every hour. Don't let the water get above 4°C/40°F.

### 5 SHARPEN YOUR KNIVES.
Blunt knives are much more dangerous than sharp knives because they force you to apply too much pressure, which can lead to slips and cuts. So get a sharpening steel and use it at least once a week.

### 6 REMEMBER THAT RECIPE TIMES ARE SUGGESTIONS, NOT GUARANTEES.
Your smoker may be a little hotter than mine. The roast from my fridge may have been a little cooler than yours. Mine was thicker, but yours weighed more. You may be smoking at a higher altitude than I am. All these things affect timing, so use the recipes as guides, but then verify the desired doneness by inserting an instant-read meat thermometer into the centre of the meat, not touching a bone.

## GUIDELINESS FOR DONENESS

For optimal safety, the official guidelines recommend cooking red meat to 63°C/145°F (final temperature) and minced red meat to 75°C/167°F. A temperature of 63°C/145°F is officially defined as medium rare, but virtually all chefs today believe medium rare is closer to 55°C/130°F. The chart right compares chef standards with official recommendations. Ultimately, doneness decisions are your choice.

| DONENESS | CHEF STANDARDS | OFFICIAL GUIDELINES |
|---|---|---|
| **RED MEAT:** Rare | 49–55°C/120–125°F | n/a |
| **RED MEAT:** Medium rare | 55–60°C/125–135°F | 63°C/145°F |
| **RED MEAT:** Medium | 60–63°C/135–145°F | 70°C/160°F |
| **RED MEAT:** Medium well | 63–68°C/145–155°F | n/a |
| **RED MEAT:** Well done | 68°C/155°F + | 77°C/170°F |
| **PORK** | 63–65°C/145–150°F | 70–75°C/145–160°F |
| **POULTRY** | 75–80°C/160–165°F | 75°C/165°F |

# CONVERSION TABLES

## CUP EQUIVALENTS FOR DIFFERENT TYPES OF INGREDIENTS

A standard cup measure of a dry or solid ingredient will vary in weight depending on the type of ingredient. A standard cup of liquid is the same volume for any type of liquid. Use the following chart when converting grams (weight) or millilitres (volume) to standard cup measures.

| STANDARD CUP | FINE POWDER (e.g. flour) | GRAIN (e.g. rice) | GRANULAR (e.g. sugar) | LIQUID SOLIDS (e.g. butter) | LIQUID (e.g. milk) |
|---|---|---|---|---|---|
| ⅛ | 15 g | 25 g | 25 g | 35 g | 30 ml |
| ¼ | 25 g | 50 g | 50 g | 60 g | 60 ml |
| ⅓ | 40 g | 75 g | 75 g | 80 g | 80 ml |
| ½ | 50 g | 100 g | 100 g | 125 g | 120 ml |
| ⅔ | 80 g | 125 g | 150 g | 160 g | 160 ml |
| ¾ | 90 g | 150 g | 175 g | 180 g | 180 ml |
| 1 | 125 g | 200 g | 225 g | 250 g | 240 ml |

## USEFUL EQUIVALENTS FOR LIQUID INGREDIENTS BY VOLUME

| | | | | |
|---|---|---|---|---|
| ¼ teaspoon | | | = | 1 ml |
| ½ teaspoon | | | = | 2 ml |
| 1 teaspoon | | | = | 5 ml |
| 3 teaspoons = 1 tablespoon | | = ½ fl oz | = | 15 ml |
| | 2 tablespoons | = ⅛ cup = 1 fl oz | = | 30 ml |
| | 4 tablespoons | = ¼ cup = 2 fl oz | = | 60 ml |
| | 5⅓ tablespoons | = ⅓ cup = 3 fl oz | = | 80 ml |
| | 8 tablespoons | = ½ cup = 4 fl oz | = | 120 ml |
| | 10⅔ tablespoons | = ⅔ cup = 5 fl oz | = | 160 ml |
| | 12 tablespoons | = ¾ cup = 6 fl oz | = | 180 ml |
| | 16 tablespoons | = 1 cup = 8 fl oz | = | 240 ml |
| | | 2½ cups = 1 pint | = | 480 ml |
| | | = 4 cups = 1¾ pints | = | 1 litre |

## USEFUL EQUIVALENTS FOR DRY INGREDIENTS BY WEIGHT

To convert grams to ounces, divide the number of grams by 30.

| | | |
|---|---|---|
| 1 oz | = ¹⁄₁₆ lb | = 30 g |
| 4 oz | = ¼ lb | = 120 g |
| 8 oz | = ½ lb | = 240 g |
| 12 oz | = ¾ lb | = 360 g |
| 16 oz | = 1 lb | = 480 g |

## USEFUL EQUIVALENTS FOR LENGTH

To convert centimeters to inches, divide the number of centimetrEs by 2.5.

| |
|---|
| 1 inch = 2.5 cm |
| 6 inches = ½ foot = 15 cm |
| 12 inches = 1 foot = 30 cm |
| 36 inches = 3 feet = 1 yard = 90 cm |
| 40 inches = 100 cm =1 metre |

## USEFUL EQUIVALENTS FOR COOKING/OVEN TEMPERATURES

| | FAHRENHEIT | CELSIUS | GAS MARK |
|---|---|---|---|
| Freezing point | 32°F | 0°C | |
| Room temperature | 68°F | 20°C | |
| Boiling point | 212°F | 100°C | |
| Bake | 325°F | 160°C | 3 |
| | 350°F | 180°C | 4 |
| | 375°F | 190°C | 5 |
| | 400°F | 200°C | 6 |
| | 425°F | 220°C | 7 |
| | 450°F | 230°C | 8 |

# INDEX

# TUVWZ

AN HACHETTE UK COMPANY
www.hachette.co.uk

First published in Great Britain in 2013 by Hamlyn,
an imprint of Octopus Publishing Group Ltd
Carmelite House
50 Victoria Embankment
London EC4Y 0DZ
www.octopusbooks.co.uk

The authorized representative in the EEA is Hachette Ireland, 8 Castlecourt Centre,
Dublin 15, D15 XTP3, Ireland (email: info@hbgi.ie)

This edition published in 2017

ISBN-13: 978-0-600-63512-3

A CIP catalogue record for this book is available from the British Library

Printed and bound in China

10 9 8 7 6

www.weber.com®
www.sunset.com

MIX
Paper | Supporting
responsible forestry
FSC
www.fsc.org
FSC® C008047

Author: Jamie Purviance

Managing Editor (US edition): Marsha Capen
Photography: Tim Turner
Food Styling: Lynn Gagné
Illustrations: Keith Witmer
Weber-Stephens Products LLC Mike Kempster, Chief Marketing Officer
Round Mountain Media Susan Maruyama, Consultant Publishing Director
Oxmoor House Jim Childs, Vice President and Publishing Director

Commissioning Editor (UK edition): Eleanor Maxfield
Design: theoakstudio.co.uk
Editor: Jo Wilson
Production Manager: Peter Hunt

Images courtesy Weber-Stephens Products LLC, 2013, except for the following:-
Beech chippings page 21 courtesy smokedust.co.uk